Best wishes D2
from Freda 1982

D0590284

# MY GREATEST
# TRAINING TRIUMPH

*Also by John Hughes*

MY GREATEST RACE (editor)

# MY GREATEST TRAINING TRIUMPH

*Edited by*
JOHN HUGHES and PETER WATSON

*With a Foreword by*
Brough Scott

LONDON
MICHAEL JOSEPH

First published in Great Britain by
Michael Joseph Limited
44 Bedford Square
London WC1
1982

© This collection by John Hughes 1982

All Rights Reserved. No part of this publication
may be reproduced, stored in a retrieval system,
or transmitted, in any form or by any means,
electronic, mechanical, photocopying, recording
or otherwise without the prior permission
of the Copyright owner.

ISBN 0 7181 2172 4

Typeset by Rowland Phototypesetting Limited,
Bury St Edmunds, Suffolk
Printed and bound in Great Britain
by Fakenham Press Limited,
Fakenham, Norfolk

# Contents

Foreword by Brough Scott                    9

Ian Balding                                11
Arthur Budgett                             20
Henry Cecil                                27
Neville Crump                              33
Michael Dickinson                          38
John Dunlop                                48
Peter Easterby                             55
Tim Forster                                61
Josh Gifford                               68
Guy Harwood                                82
Criquette Head                             91
Barry Hills                                97
Arthur Moore                              103
Sir Noel Murless                          110
Vincent O'Brien                           116
Mick O'Toole                              123
Ryan Price                                128
Fred Rimell                               134
Michael Stoute                            144
Jeremy Tree                               150
Fulke Walwyn                              156
Peter Walwyn                              162
Dermot Weld                               170
Fred Winter                               176

Index                                     187

# Acknowledgements

Our warmest thanks to each and every trainer for the time and trouble they took in helping us compile what we feel is a unique collection of stories; our thanks also to the photographers and photographic agencies for their help in illustrating the book, and to Brough Scott for his generous foreword. Finally, but by no means least, our appreciation to those magnificent horses without which there would be no story at all.

John Hughes and Peter Watson

The Trustees of the Apprentice School Charitable Trust gratefully acknowledge the authors', editors' and publishers' generous contribution by way of part of the proceeds from the sale of this book towards the establishment of a training centre for stable staff and apprentice jockeys.

*Photographic Acknowledgements*

The editors would like to thank all the trainers who supplied photographs from their private collections; in addition, they would like to thank the following for other photographs which appear in this book. The folios refer to the pages on which they are printed.

Syndication International: 10, 76, 168, 184. Keystone Press Agency: 17, 24, 51, 136, 141, 142. Colorlabs International Ltd: 18. BBC Hulton Picture Library: 28, 62, 117, 119, 164. Tony Jakobson: 30. Selwyn Photos: 31, 44, 47, 57, 59, 70, 93, 160. S & G Press Agency Ltd: 35, 84, 87, 88, 98, 111, 112, 114, 121, 126, 129, 153, 154, 158, 167, 173, 174, 182. The Press Association Ltd: 53. Gerry Cranham: 18. Patricia Smyly: 66. W. Everitt: 80, 100, 101. APRH, P. Bertrand & Fils: 94, 95. Ruth Rogers: 107, 124, 171. Peter Mooney: 108. Colin Sims: 132. Popperfoto: 139. Alec Russell: 147. Fox Photos: 178.

# Foreword
## by Brough Scott

When it comes to secrets, racehorse trainers are almost as coveted as call girls' address books. Trust John Hughes to get them (the trainers) to talk.

For this book is an original, an open window into a normally mysterious world where reports are apt to come trickling in about eighteenth hand and often laden with the prejudices of whichever of us hacks is telling the tale.

These are not the normal snatched phrases as the trainer pauses before hustling the owners off to the bar. They are detailed enough for the confessional and confirm something that many have long suspected—that racehorse trainers are the most neurotic bunch of perfectionists that ever graced the kingdom.

Hughes and Peter Watson record how Henry Cecil thought Le Moss might pull up in the middle of the Gold Cup, how John Dunlop discovered that Shirley Heights was 'remarkably unfit', how Josh Gifford thought Aldaniti much too slow to be a racehorse and how Michael Dickinson used a magic sweet to calm the lunatic tendencies of Silver Buck.

My only complaint is that while the trainers correctly emerge from these pages as obsessive, caring saints, they also appear as even-tempered peacemakers—and we all know this not to be the case. Racehorse training and the frustration of watching a horse you have spent years developing running out, away, or just plain badly, has driven strong men to tears, has made Peter Walwyn hit his head against a wall and, when I was riding for him, used to make Colin Davies throw his cap on the ground and jump on it in fury.

So we look forward to Hughes' and Watson's next collection of trainers' tales—'My greatest rollocking'! But for the moment, the following chapters take you right inside the four-legged world. They are in simple terms the racing junkies' ultimate fix.

# IAN BALDING

Longchamp on Arc de Triomphe day has a very special air of excitement and expectation and to my mind it ranks very highly in the list of international sporting occasions. When Mill Reef set out on Sunday 3 October 1971 to try to become the first English-trained winner of the great race for twenty-three years, I was very nervous indeed. The racing public had taken him to their hearts and I felt an enormous sense of responsibility. There was the same very hollow feeling in my stomach which I can only remember experiencing once before—when I ran onto the pitch for Cambridge at Twickenham in the 1961 Varsity Rugby Match.

The Arc has always seemed to me to be the most competitive race of the year in Europe and coming as it does at the end of the season, when a classic three-year-old can so easily be past its best, it presents a considerable test for any trainer. So even with Mill Reef to work with, it was a tremendous challenge in only my seventh full season as a trainer.

But frankly, when I first set eyes on Mill Reef in November 1969, I certainly did not envisage making that journey with him. Bred by his owner Paul Mellon at his lovely Rokeby Farm in Virginia, Mill Reef was by the very speedy Never Bend out of Milan Mill, a daughter of Princequillo who traced back to that good English mare Red Ray. In subsequent years, I have made an annual trip to Rokeby to help select the yearlings which Mr Mellon sends to England. At that time, however, I had nothing to do with the selection of Mill Reef coming over and for that vital and, for me, fortuitous decision I have to thank not only Mr Mellon but also the influence of Preston Burch, who thought apparently that the colt's rather long sloping pasterns would be more suited to the turf courses of England than to the American dirt tracks.

The next important decision in the horse's career was that John Hallum chose to look after him rather than the bigger and more flashy looking colt of Mr Mellon's called Quantico, who came over in the same batch of

*Opposite page*
Mill Reef

yearlings. John is without doubt the best stable lad I have so far encountered and much as one tries to see that your best lads 'do' what you think may be the best horses, it doesn't always work out that way. In the same week that Mill Reef arrived, my old friend Bill Palmer, who had been stable jockey for my brother Toby and had recently retired from the saddle, came to Kingsclere to take over as head lad. I am certain that his dedication as well as John's played a very big part in Mill Reef's success.

The first thing that struck me about Mill Reef was his colour—a lovely deep mahogany bay and even in mid-winter his coat had a gleam to it that was remarkable. He was, however, very small and rather set, so that one could dream perhaps that he might be a very fast early two-year-old but certainly not at that stage a future Derby winner. The other feature about him that was immediately noticeable was his beautiful easy light action. Right from his earliest days, he seemed to float along when others with a more rounded action were labouring around him.

When we started to do a little bit more with the two-year-olds than just canter, he looked at once to be in a different class from the others and, by March, I was thinking that either he was exceptional or the others were totally useless. As it turned out both surmises were correct. He had one good gallop before the Salisbury Stakes on 13 May 1970 with Red Reef whom he left over twenty lengths behind. I don't think I ever worked him with another two-year-old again after that. He was our first two-year-old runner of the year so although we were all very hopeful about his chances, we had no form line to go on. He started at 8–1 with the previous impressive winner Fireside Chat at 9–2 on. Mill Reef flew out of the stalls, was never headed, and won very easily. The guessing had ended and we now knew we had at Kingsclere an exceptional two-year-old.

He won the Coventry Stakes at Royal Ascot in a common canter and because, at this stage, I felt we had a flying two-year-old who probably would not train on, I decided to send him to France for the very valuable Prix Robert Papin. After a ghastly journey over, which contributed towards him eating hardly anything for the two days before the race, he was beaten a short head by My Swallow. He was drawn on the wide outside which at Maisons-Laffitte is a considerable disadvantage, and he seemed in every way a very unlucky loser.

He had had a hard race, too, and when a month later Mr Mellon came to see him run for the first time in the Gimcrack at York on 20 August, I lost my nerve and did my best to stop him running in the very heavy ground. Luckily Mr Mellon's wisdom prevailed and his ten-length win from Green God that day remains for me the most impressive performance by a two-year-old I have ever seen. He went on to win the Imperial Stakes at Kempton by a length and the Dewhurst, being ridden from behind for the first time, very easily.

When one thinks of the other great mile-and-a-half champions of recent times, such as Sea Bird, Nijinsky, Grundy, Troy and Shergar, none showed Mill Reef's speed as a two-year-old and one would probably have to go back a long way to find another Derby winner who won over five furlongs in the May of his two-year-old season. So perhaps I could be forgiven for thinking during the winter that we had an outstanding Two Thousand Guineas prospect rather than a Derby or an Arc horse.

I felt that I would never have a better chance of winning a Classic than the 1971 Two Thousand Guineas and was determined to have Mill Reef as fit as he could be for that day. Therefore, he had a preliminary outing in the Greenham Stakes at Newbury on 17 April which he won very impressively giving us all a great deal of confidence. My Swallow had won his trial just as easily but I felt we had the beating of him, and the nigger in the woodpile could be Brigadier Gerard who was to come to the big day without a previous run. I knew Dick Hern would have him ready to run for his life but I thought our two-year-old form was just better and that Brigadier Gerard would have to have made abnormal improvement during the winter to beat us.

The Brigadier's comprehensive win is now history and the race remains as one of the biggest disappointments of my life. I was not to know at the time, of course, that we were encountering probably the greatest miler of them all, or indeed that it was not to be Mill Reef's proper distance. The only consolation perhaps was Geoff Lewis's firm conviction later that nothing would beat us in the Derby, and that the way our little horse stayed on up the hill, he would get the trip at Epsom.

I was not so sure but fortunately had the sense not to try to find out at home before Derby Day. His one decent bit of work between the Two Thousand Guineas and the Derby was over 1¼ miles but it was more a case of covering the ground and quickening up the last three furlongs than a proper trial gallop. He finished impressively but on the big day I was still hopeful rather than confident. I cannot claim to have given Mill Reef a marvellous preparation for the Derby—all I can say perhaps is that I did not overtrain him.

It was, of course, a great thrill to win the Derby, but my nerves were not helped by being caught in a traffic jam and having to run the last two miles in my tails and topper! My wife Emma and I also missed some of the post-race euphoria by having to fly to the U.S.A. for my sister's wedding that same evening. The race itself went remarkably smoothly. Geoff always had Mill Reef in the right position and he beat Linden Tree comfortably in the end, but not impressively. Most significantly though he stayed really well, and instead of fearing that we might merely have the second-best miler in the country, I suddenly realised that the great middle-distance races of Europe might be within our grasp.

I chose the Eclipse Stakes over 1¼ miles at Sandown as his next race rather than the Irish Derby, partly because I was still anxious not to travel him abroad again until absolutely necessary and also because I felt the distance and timing of the race made it a more suitable build-up for the King George VI and Queen Elizabeth II Stakes at Ascot, which had now to be the ultimate mid-summer target.

Fortunately, Mill Reef really thrived after the Derby. The warmer weather seemed to do wonders for him and at Sandown on 3 July he looked a much bigger, stronger horse than he had a month earlier at Epsom. We had bought a good pace-maker in Bright Beam who was now ridden by Geoff's great friend, Tommy Carter, who was himself a fine judge of pace. He did his job well enabling the little horse to settle down some way off the lead. It was most exciting when Mill Reef and the excellent French-trained four-year-old, Caro, suddenly went clear from the rest of the field with a quarter of a mile to run. It was quite breathtaking when Mill Reef found yet another gear in the last furlong and drew right away from his rival to win by four lengths. He not only broke the track record but was going so fast at the finish that he would have won by eight or ten lengths if the race had been another furlong. I realise I am biased, but I think that anyone who saw Mill Reef that day witnessed a super horse at his peak.

We ran our pace-maker again in the King George three weeks later, but obviously some of the senior jockeys were still not convinced that Mill Reef was a genuine stayer, and they went so fast early on in the race that Bright Beam could not, or indeed had any need to, augment the pace. All his rivals seemed exhausted by the time they reached the straight and Mill Reef sauntered away to win by six lengths with Geoff scarcely having to move a muscle.

Now it was decision time. Did we aim for the St Leger or the Arc or both? Up to now, the races had almost picked themselves and the preparation of the horse had been relatively straightforward. I felt that my real test as a trainer was only just starting.

Mr Mellon and I were both very keen to win the Arc; we felt it was not just the most valuable and prestigious race of the year in Europe, but also the ultimate test for the true middle-distance champion. Much as I would love to have won the St Leger—and I was quite certain Mill Reef could have won it had we let him run—I did not feel it fitted into his programme if we wanted to win the Arc. Admittedly, we were not chasing the Triple Crown as Nijinsky had been the previous year, but it was still a difficult decision to make, to deliberately miss a Classic in which our horse would have started about 8–1 on!

There were ten weeks between the King George and the Arc and I felt it was vital to give him a four-week rest after Ascot which thus allowed him a six-week build-up for the big race at Longchamp. If one had considered using the St Leger as a preparatory race for the Arc, it would have given us only three weeks to train Mill Reef for what was after all a Classic; also the distance of 1¾ miles was, in my opinion, hardly suitable as a stepping stone for the 1½ miles test three weeks later. Ideally, I would have liked a race over 1¼ miles about two weeks before the Arc and an easy confidence-building race at that. There was nothing suitable at that time, so we took him to Newbury racecourse for a decent work-out with Morris Dancer and Bright Beam over 1¼ miles. Although there was no prize money, it seemed ideal.

Now about his four-week rest period after Ascot: what exactly does one mean by rest? One cannot suddenly turn out into a paddock a fit, fresh, three-year-old colt worth several million pounds as one might do with a filly. Nor can one afford to 'let him down' in condition as one does for example during the winter months. I considered that a break, mentally as well as physically was needed and more than anything perhaps a change in routine. Consequently, I sent him off with my great stable servant Aldie, a grand horse, for light exercise on their own. It was here that the beauty of Kingsclere as a training establishment with its vast variety of gallops helped. Instead of going to the Downs twice a week, the two of them would go for a jog and steady canter on the winter gallops we had not used for six months, or wander round the farm right away from the main string. Then every evening, John Hallum would take him out for a long lead and pick of grass insead of being tied up and rigorously groomed at evening stables. All this time, however, Bill Palmer scarcely had to cut down on his feed at all. We did just enough exercise with him to stop him getting too fresh for safety, but always right away from the main summer gallops.

All seemed to go smoothly, but in spite of my careful planning, I still had an uneasy feeling that perhaps the horse might just have gone over the top. His work after the Newbury gallop seemed to lack sparkle and I could just begin to detect his coat losing a little of its summer bloom. Geoff shared my anxiety and I must say those last two weeks became somewhat testing for us all.

I was determined that nothing should be left to chance when it came to travelling. We hired a big Brittania jet to ourselves and received permission, with some difficulty, to fly direct from the American air base at Greenham

Common just three miles away to Le Bourget. The customs and general clearance procedures were all completed before Mill Reef even left his box at Kingsclere. Emma and I travelled with him, along with John Hallum, our travelling head lad Bill Jennings, also old Aldie with his lad Mick Weedy for company, and Tom Reilly the stable blacksmith. We were a determined team, but not by any means over-confident.

Within two hours of leaving his own box, Mill Reef was safely installed in a beautifully isolated little stable called La Camargo at Lamorlaye on the Thursday before the race. Aldie was in the box next to him and the four men in a spacious flat above the stable. Emma and I stayed about a mile away at an attractive little hotel in a village called Coye-le-Forêt. Mill Reef and Aldie had a jog and steady canter the next day and a nice long lead and pick of grass in the evening. Then on the Saturday morning, the day before the big race, he had his final work-out—a sharp spin over four furlongs on the lovely grass training grounds nearby.

It was then that I really discovered the possible explanation for Mill Reef's amazing aptitude for soft ground. There were a couple of quite heavy patches on the ground we used which generally one might describe as good to soft. I remember walking up afterwards between the little markers where the horses had worked and Aldie, who was a genuine top-of-the-ground horse with a light daisy-cutting action himself, had gone in quite deep. One could plainly see his tracks all the way up, and through the two heavy patches he had turned the turf right over. There were virtually no marks at all where Mill Reef had been and through the two heavy patches he had made about as much imprint as Aldie had on the good bit of ground. It was almost as if a phantom horse had been there and showed us what an amazing action Mill Reef had. The work itself was just what we all needed—whether the horse did or not. He went quite brilliantly in the unfamiliar surroundings and wouldn't have blown out a candle afterwards. It certainly restored most of our confidence.

The big day arrived and we travelled in our little car behind the French horsebox from Lamorlaye to Longchamp. I remember worrying how unnecessarily fast the box was going, but still they arrived safely. We were very early and, to soothe the nerves a bit, I walked round the course which was in superb condition. Longchamp suddenly seemed to fill up very quickly. There were hundreds of English supporters, most of whom appeared to have been given a Mill Reef lapel badge in Mr Mellon's black and gold colours by my brother-in-law, William Hastings-Bass, himself a successful trainer now. The atmosphere was electric—more akin to that just before a Rugby Football international than a race day. Although Mill Reef was owned and bred by an American, he was running for England that day

*Opposite page*
*Magnifique!* Geoff Lewis and Mill Reef win the 1971 Arc in record-breaking time

Ian Balding renews
acquaintances with
Mill Reef at the
National Stud

and even the French, who love a great horse, had come, not just to support their own horses, but also to admire him.

I remember well the spontaneous clapping that broke out as the little horse appeared in the paddock. Luckily Mill Reef took that in his stride as he did the rest of the preliminaries and his superb temperament must have helped the jockey relax, even if it didn't rid the trainer of his nerves.

The main worry in the race itself would be whether, or where, Geoff would get a clear run from behind. He looked always to be running in about fourth position until just before turning into the straight where he seemed to lose his place briefly and, for a ghastly moment, I lost him altogether and thought he must have been swept back in behind the early leaders who were rapidly losing their places. For an agonising second, I even thought he might have fallen, as, straining to see over the constantly moving, excited French heads in the trainers' stand, I struggled to see at all.

Then, thank goodness for that white sheepskin noseband I put on all my runners; suddenly, I could see it darting through a narrow gap on the rails. One smack from Geoff and Mill Reef was away. Fast though Pistol Packer finished, that brilliant filly of Alec Head's had no chance of catching him. Mill Reef won by three lengths and again broke the track record.

Geoff and Mill Reef received a fantastic reception. We were immediately whisked away to meet the French President and receive our trophies, and to see endless replays of the race. Later, the hordes of noisy, but happy, English visitors, with their Mill Reef badges now very evident, seemed to have taken over the whole area around the paddock and weighing room. With empty bottles of champagne everywhere and lots of singing, one had no doubt whose 'team' had won this 'match'.

Mr Mellon gave a dinner party later at the Crillon Hotel and we stayed the night in Paris, thus having the chance to reflect and savour what I feel will always be the happiest and most satisfying moment of my training career.

I could not finish without paying tribute both to Mr Mellon and my great friend Geoff Lewis. Mr Mellon is quite simply the best owner one could have. He seemed happy to leave all the decisions to me and gave me the best present I could wish, a marvellous bronze sculpture of Mill Reef by John Skeaping which stands today in the centre of the new yard.

Geoff rode Mill Reef in all his races and in most of his serious home gallops as well. If, in our early days together, through my inexperience and Geoff's somewhat impetuous nature, we lost some big races that perhaps we should have won, he for one learned from those near misses. If Mill Reef was ever in the wrong place throughout any of his races, I can't recall it. I remember Geoff's dedication in driving down from Epsom twice a week all through that summer, even though he was having to go to Newmarket on the other mornings. I remember him cutting out all drink and cigarettes for ten days before each big race. I remember his encouragement and wise counsel. Most of the great horses of our time seem to have been ridden by Lester Piggott, but in my opinion not even that genius could have ridden Mill Reef with more consistent brilliance than Geoff did, and I shall always be grateful for the very considerable part he played in my Greatest Training Triumph.

# ARTHUR BUDGETT

When Morston won the Derby at Epsom on Wednesday 6 June 1973 on only his second racecourse appearance, I couldn't help reflecting on a day at the 1961 Tattersalls December Sales . . .

Peter Towers-Clark, my Stud Manager at the Kirtlington Stud, and I had hoped to buy a foal by Lord Astor's St Leger runner-up Hornbeam out of a staying mare called Chorus Beauty bred by Major Lionel Holliday. As fillies from this family were nearly unobtainable—she went back on her dam's side to Fancy Free, dam of the Derby winner Blue Peter and the line was full of winners—we thought it most unlikely that she would come within our price range. She caused no stir whatsoever in the sale ring and was led out unsold behind her dam. We decided immediately to offer the reserve price of 1,000 guineas and Peter succeeded in completing the deal in a very short time. I could not anticipate then how much that purchase was going to mean to me.

She was to be named Windmill Girl after the famous theatre chorus, and she went on to finish second in the 1964 Oaks before winning the Ribblesdale at Royal Ascot. She produced her first foal, a bay colt by Major Holliday's horse, Heathersett—as Heathersett is the name of a village in Norfolk, that colt was named Blakeney after another Norfolk village with a famous windmill. Blakeney became my first Derby winner in 1969—and Windmill Girl had just been tested in foal to Ragusa when he won it.

Windmill Girl duly produced a fine chestnut colt at Baron Guy de Rothschild's Haras de Meautry near Deauville in Normandy and for his name, we sought a neighbouring village to Blakeney. Morston sounded a suitable name for a Derby winner, so Morston it was, although nobody concerned had even been there, or to Blakeney for that matter. Harry Deacon, our stud groom, who had reared Windmill Girl and Blakeney, became very ill and died when Morston was a foal. His loving care and attention was sadly missed.

Arthur Budgett with
Morston

When Morston went into training as a yearling, he soon showed in his
early canters that he was a beautiful mover and had a good turn of foot.
However, he was backward and it was decided that he would not be trained
seriously until the back end of his two-year-old career. When the time came,
he contracted a cough and, although it had been hoped to give him the
experience of a run in the autumn, it was clearly unwise to risk a colt of his
potential by running him in below peak condition. Derby Day at Epsom the
following June was the day that mattered. There was no anxious owner to
worry about, so Morston went in to winter quarters without a run.

Although he did well, he was still backward the following spring and as
the going was heavy and he had suffered another but minor bout of
coughing, the preparation was not hurried.

One morning, while he was doing a steady half-speed on Summer Down,
he suddenly playfully grabbed the boot of the rider of the horse which was
working up-sides him. Clearly, he was fooling about and not paying
attention to his work. Something had to be done about it and so I asked

Tom Dowdeswell, our head lad, then aged sixty-three, if he would ride him in his future work. Tom had a childhood background in the hunting field and a wide experience of riding work on high class horses. He possesses that rare quality of having a great affinity with, and understanding of, the horse which he is riding. He jumped at the idea and the transformation in Morston was startling.

It soon became clear that he was a cut above the ordinary and could even be another Blakeney. As yet, he had not been asked the question, but had shown glimpses of that fantastic turn of foot without which a horse would be lucky to win a Derby. His gradual preparation was carefully worked out and, if all went well, it was hoped that there would be just time for him to have a race in the Lingfield Derby Trial on 12 May before the Derby itself.

Then one morning, conceding a good deal of weight to another useful horse, he had a harder gallop than had been intended. For the first time, he went off his feed and the damage done was all too apparent at evening stables. If his planned programme of work was interrupted now, would he be fit to run in the Derby and, if it was not, would he be in any state to win the Derby? I decided to put him on the easy list until he came back on to his full feed; this took about ten days. He had an alternative entry to the Derby Trial—also at Lingfield, which is so similar to Epsom—in the Godstone Plate, a maiden race of 1¼ miles. I thought that might give him an easier introduction to racing. Morston made remarkable progress but Epsom was drawing nearer and I decided that, as a hard race in the Derby Trial would most probably be fatal to any chance he might have in the big race itself, he would run in the maiden instead.

By then, he was clearly back in form and eating everything that was put in front of him. There was a field of fourteen runners; although he had been trained at home to work through other horses, the experience of being boxed in, in a race, was thought to be essential for his Derby preparation. Frankie Durr was engaged to ride him with instructions that, although we hoped he would win, his preparation had been interrupted and whatever happened he was not to be given a hard race. He was in good hands; Frankie had Morston in a good position all the way, took the lead over two furlongs out, and won convincingly by three lengths. He swerved over to the stands in the last furlong—due to greenness, according to Frankie—but at no stage had he been able to taste the experience of being boxed in amongst the other horses; nonetheless, Frankie advised me to run him in the Derby.

His stable companion and our main Derby hope, Projector, with whom he had worked well in half-speed gallops at home, ran a most promising race in the Derby Trial the following day and was beaten half a length by the favourite Ksar. That earned Projector a quote of 100–8 for the Derby. The two horses had not done more than half-speed work together because Morston's preparation had been interrupted, and to have tried them between Lingfield and Epsom would have taken the edge off both for the big race. It was not easy, therefore, to forecast which was going to be the better on the day. There was no doubt that Morston had the makings of a great horse but he lacked experience and was still virtually untried.

Then Julian Wilson rang asking to come to Whatcombe on a Friday morning twelve days before the Derby to take some film of Projector for the BBC Television Derby Preview programme. This was arranged for the first lot, but it was discovered too late to stop the camera crew, that Projector had been cast in his box in the night; he was slightly lame and would not be able to do exercise that morning. Julian decided that, as everything was in readiness and on the spot, Morston should be filmed instead. The camera was set up on Wolley Downs—and Morston was almost upstaged by Grock, our old dog. He had a particularly photogenic and aristocratic profile, unfortunately belied by his pedigree, and the whirring camera as he trotted proudly by appeared to suggest that he was creating a greater interest than the Derby candidate. Julian was most impressed, however, when Morston swept by and mentioned that he had never yet failed to show the Derby winner among the eight horses which he had selected each year. Morston duly appeared instead of Projector among Julian's eight.

By now our top security precautions had been put into action to cover both Derby candidates. Wynnie Maxwell, widow of trainer Bob Maxwell, an old friend of mine, and her daughter Diana were ensconced in a caravan. When Wynnie appeared in my old Army greatcoat with a loaded 4.10 at the ready, they were promptly dubbed Mums' Army by the lads. After all, Dad's Army with their shotguns and pitchforks had put the wind up Hitler and Wynnie looked just as formidable!

Projector made a quick recovery; he was approaching his peak and a couple of days off had done him no harm. Some thought that he was the better of the two; most felt it would be little short of a miracle if Morston, with unorthodox preparations and lack of experience, could win. I hoped Projector would acquit himself well and be thereabouts at the finish— especially after his promising performance at Lingfield—but he had never shown that real spark of brilliance which was a prerequisite of a Derby winner. Although the temptation to subject Morston to a trial at home had been resisted, he had given me the impression confirmed by Tom Dowdeswell and Frankie Durr, that he might well have that spark, and the fact that he had not had a trial just as he was rapidly gaining strength, had enabled him to develop his physique to the maximum possible by Derby Day. I just hoped for the miracle.

I had been lucky enough to obtain Edward Hide at the last moment to ride Morston. Colonel Percy Wright, the owner of Projector, held a retainer on Geoff Baxter. I did not have to worry how Percy Wright would take it if Morston did happen to beat Projector; after many happy years training for him, I could be sure that there would be no recriminations from that quarter.

We had taken Geoff Baxter to see films of Lester Piggott's Derbys which his father Keith very kindly offered to show—as indeed he had done for Ernie Johnson before Blakeney's Derby. This had helped us considerably to work out our tactics when Blakeney was drawn No. 1, supposedly the most disadvantageous of all on that occasion.

The horses breezed in great style over two and a half furlongs on the day before the race, and cleaned up their feed that night and their early breakfast. They seemed, and looked, to be on top of their form and they were boxed for Epsom under the care of Peter Maughan, the head travelling lad, and Tony Kirby who did Projector, and Derek Guy who did Morston. Both could certainly feel proud of the far from unimportant part they had played in the proceedings.

The horses travelled well to Epsom and looked a credit in the paddock to the work the lads had put in on them. I told Edward Hide that I thought Morston might be a great horse in the making and that, much as I would like to win the Derby again, whatever happened he was not to hurt him. Edward noticed that Morston was No. 13 on the racecard and his thirteenth ride in a race he had never won; rumour has it that Edward said to another jockey on the way to the start that he did not know why he had come to ride a non-trier when he could have ridden four good things at Ripon that afternoon!

Frankie Durr was on the Two Thousand Guineas winner Mon Fils, who started second favourite to Ksar with Morston somewhat surprisingly more fancied than Projector in the betting at 25–1 with Projector 28–1. Frankie set out to try to make all the running and Edward was in the middle of the field near the rails as they came down Tattenham Corner. Ksar was just ahead of Morston with Lester Piggott on Cavo Doro just outside Ksar. Sadly, Projector was struck into and the plate on his near hind was half wrenched off—that finished his chances; Mon Fils looked in trouble over a quarter of a mile from home and Freefoot, ridden by Pat Eddery, took the lead with Ksar improving and Edward and Morston sitting comfortably on his tail. Edward asked Morston to go one and a half furlongs out—and he went, running straight as a barrel while Lester and Cavo Doro hung in behind; no horse could have responded more gamely and nobody could have ridden a better race than Edward. Morston comfortably held off Cavo

*Opposite page*
Morston receives a well-earned pat from Edward Hide after winning the Derby

Doro by half a length without being hurt or hit.

My wife, Bay, and our fifteen-year-old son Christopher, who was on leave from school, hurried down to greet Morston. Windmill Girl had become the first mare in the twentieth century to breed two Derby winners; I had become the first Englishman in the history of the race to own, breed and train two colts to win two Derbys . . . and Julian Wilson had maintained his record!

# HENRY CECIL

Anyone who saw Le Moss work at Newmarket would have laughed at the idea of him being a top-class racehorse; I never had a horse so lazy and stubborn at home to be such an honest, tough campaigner on the racecourse.

Personal satisfaction must be the key to any triumph and although I am reluctant to pinpoint a certain horse when so many have helped me reap the glory, Le Moss's second successive Ascot Gold Cup on Thursday 19 June 1980, when he had not had a previous race that season, undoubtedly gave me most pleasure although I feel he must have been an extraordinary and exceptional horse to have achieved that victory with or without the help of my staff at Warren Place or myself.

But then he was an extraordinary horse; a full brother to the Arc de Triomphe and Ascot Gold Cup winner Levmoss, he was bought for 26,000 guineas as a yearling by one of my owners, Carlo d'Alassio, off his own bat from the Brownstown Stud in Ireland. Le Moss was always a very imposing horse and when I went over to Ireland to see him, I remember thinking that he didn't walk very well but he walked away with a certain swagger, a certain air, with his tail going like a pendulum. 'Yes,' I told Mr d'Alassio, 'I'd like to have a try with him.'

That turned out to be something of a trying time for he was very backward as a two-year-old and we didn't run him until the Dorking Maiden Stakes at Sandown on 19 October 1977; he was last into the straight but ran on to be seventh in a field of twenty-four and, considering just how backward he was, we were pretty encouraged. He always looked as though he might make into a nice stayer in time.

Le Moss won his maiden at Newmarket in May the following year before demonstrating that toughness for the first time on the racecourse when he won the 2-mile Queen's Vase at Royal Ascot on 21 June, getting up in the

The winning smile of
Henry Cecil

last strides to beat Antler. Victories at Ayr and Goodwood were followed by second place to Julio Mariner in the St Leger.

And so to 1979 and the unhappiest victory of my career; sorry if that sounds slightly zany, but Le Moss's Ascot Gold Cup win that year really was a very sad occasion for he beat his stable companion Buckskin who had been kept in training as a six-year-old with only this race in mind. Buckskin was a brilliant horse plagued with leg trouble; we had nursed him through the Doncaster Cup and Jockey Club Cup the previous year after taking him over from Peter Walwyn. He suffered from dropped soles and had to have his feet raised with special high-heeled shoes, on the outside of his off-fore his suspensory was in trouble, not only was it very sore but extremely enlarged and he spent up to two hours a day under the hose pipe.

Although Buckskin was a top-class mile-and-a-half horse who, in my opinion, could have won the King George and the Arc, we could not let down his work or sharpen him up; we just had to hold him together. He was wrapped up in cotton wool and bandaged as well. He won his warm-up race, the Henry II Stakes at Sandown in May, by fifteen lengths on the soft ground he loved and my stable jockey, Joe Mercer, out of sentiment, chose to ride him in the Gold Cup although he very much feared Le Moss. Le Moss himself had pulled a muscle in March and had just one small race at Haydock in May; Lester Piggott was asked to ride him.

Buckskin never really stayed more than two miles and the extra half-mile of the Gold Cup was too much this time; he led into the straight but Le Moss had made a move from a long way back, challenged Buckskin a furlong and a half out and went away to beat a very leg-sore and tired champion by seven heartbreaking lengths. To train and nurse a colt for the Gold Cup and end up beating him ourselves was not the happiest of occasions . . .

Le Moss went on to win the Goodwood Cup and Doncaster Cup before being beaten by Totowah in the 2-mile Jockey Club Cup at Newmarket in October, and then I resolved to prepare him to retain his crown in 1980.

That's when the fun really started; he pulled a muscle in the spring again but this time it took a long while to mend and he was in his box for six weeks. To make matters worse, he would not do his work when he finally recovered; he refused to gallop, he'd jib and stand for as long as twenty minutes at a time without jumping off. What do you do with a horse like that? When you're over a hundred in the yard—I had nearer 150 in 1982!—you're bound to have the oddball or two, and the only thing to do with Le Moss was to put a dunce's hat on him and send him off on his own. If he galloped with the maidens, he'd be beaten thirty lengths anyway, so there wasn't much point in persevering with him; we just gave up with him . . . or so he thought!

While the rest were doing their stuff, Le Moss went off on long, steady exercises by himself with a lad called Alan Welbourne riding; he seemed to enjoy this preferential treatment and strutted around the Heath but, with Alan weighing about ten and a half stone, the old horse was doing a little bit more than he thought. In the evenings, I packed him off to the Newmarket horse swimming pool; he thought that was just for his pleasure and amusement, but in fact the idea was to inject the necessary work into him.

I'd long since ruled out any idea of him having a preparatory race for the Gold Cup but decided instead to take him to Kempton and Yarmouth in the three-week period before Royal Ascot to work on a racecourse. I thought he'd at least put it in there—but he was up to our tricks, he knew it wasn't really a race, he knew there was no prize money at the end of the straight and he worked diabolically, particularly at Yarmouth where he just managed to stay with old Francesco. The trouble with horses like this is that you always fear they're going to turn it in during a race itself, that one day they'll just not bother. Horses who simply refuse to work at home, give a trainer nightmares and I was slightly nervous on Gold Cup day because I couldn't really see how Le Moss could win against the company, especially without having had a race.

Le Moss in the pool

Well, he made a monkey of everyone, making virtually every yard of the running and fighting off challenger after challenger. The French horse Croque Monsieur took him on down the back straight which was perfect for Le Moss was going slightly lazy at the time; they'd gone off at an incredible gallop and they were flat out all the way. Then Vincent came at us and finally Ardross, who was himself later to prove such a brilliant horse. Le Moss just battled away, finding that bit more than Ardross until there was three quarters of a length between them at the finish. Maybe, those long walks and daily swims had helped after all.

There's no doubt that Joe Mercer helped. He rode Le Moss magnificently; no jockey could have ridden him better and they seemed to work together with tremendous rhythm and really suited each other. Joe was unbelievable on certain horses; Kris and Light Cavalry would be two others I'd pick out and without taking anything away from Lester, I would far rather have had Joe on Light Cavalry in 1981 than Lester.

*Opposite page* Le Moss and Joe Mercer race home in the 1980 Ascot Gold Cup . . . 'they seemed to work together with tremendous rhythm,' says Henry Cecil

What, then, was the secret of Le Moss? Because we could hardly get him out of a canter at home, his physique certainly helped him; he was a slightly tubular, narrow horse, he wasn't a big gross, heavy horse. If he had been, I don't think he'd have achieved what he did for he went on from Ascot to

win both the Goodwood Cup and Doncaster Cup again before being beaten half a length by Anifa in the Prix Gladiateur at Longchamp—his final race before returning to stand at the Brownstown Stud.

My stepfather, Sir Cecil Boyd-Rochfort, was a tremendous trainer of stayers, winning the St Leger six times, the Gold Cup three times, the Goodwood Cup six times and the Doncaster Cup seven times. I feel I've picked up a lot from him, having been his assistant from 1964–68. I'm lucky, too, to have such a tremendous staff at Warren Place; basically, I leave it to them, though I'm bound to say I enjoy the sweet taste of success. I like winning and I intend to win many more major races before they put me out to grass.

# NEVILLE CRUMP

My jockey's reward for getting the mare Sheila's Cottage up in the last few yards to win the 1948 Grand National was to have the top of one of his fingers bitten off—by that very same horse!

But after over 1,000 winners in more than forty years of training, that big, strong bay holds a special place in my heart, for that victory gave me the greatest thrill of my life and changed everything for me.

At that time, I had only half a dozen horses in the yard, having moved into Warwick House at Middleham in the Yorkshire Dales after coming out of the Army in 1946. I'd first taken out a trainer's licence in 1937 but couldn't really get down to business until after the war. The locals eyed me rather warily and Swank Smith, the head lad of old Matt Peacock, greeted me with the words, 'You've got something to live up to here; we've had a second in the Grand National!'

Things didn't start too well. The first winter was hell—snow everywhere and we had no idea what we were doing. We took the horses up to Redcar and galloped them too much—and we drank too much! We made a right mess of the whole thing.

But then Sheila's Cottage came into my life. Sir Hervey Bruce, who was stationed at Catterick nearby, asked if I wanted a horse to train. He'd owned a mare by Cottage who had already sired two National winners, Workman in 1939 and Lovely Cottage in 1946 out of Sheila, who had won a few point-to-points in Ireland. Sheila's Cottage was an absolute swine, a real old brute. She'd bite and kick anybody but we soon found out she knew what she was about on the racecourse. In fact, she showed us enough to earn her chance in the 1947 National and was going well until she was knocked down at the twelfth.

We started her off at Doncaster on 14 November the next season and she was sixth in the Town Moor Handicap Chase over 3 miles. Then she won at Haydock two weeks later over 3½ miles; to my mind, that's the greatest test a horse can have for a National because of the drop fences.

Sir Hervey was delighted and we set out for Cheltenham and the 4-mile Stayers Handicap on 30 December. Hervey, who gambled a bit, asked if I thought she'd win at Cheltenham. I said, 'No, I don't think so. She'll be placed.' Sadly, Hervey didn't take me at my word; Sheila's Cottage finished third after starting 4–1 favourite and Hervey came up to me afterwards and said, 'Christ, I've done my dough—I'll have to sell the horse.'

That was very sad but I found a buyer all right—a real character called John Procter who was a trawler owner and had interests in the hotel business. Sheila's Cottage ran third at Haydock the first time she wore John's colours and then finished fifth in the Great Yorkshire Chase at Doncaster in February where the track was too fast for her.

The next stop was Aintree and the Grand National on 20 March—a day that was to change my life. Sheila's Cottage started at 50–1 in a field of forty-three and that seemed a fair reflection of her chance at the time, although I had no doubt about her ability to stay the tough 4½-mile course. Nor had I any doubt about the ability of my jockey, Arthur Thompson. He knew his way round Aintree backwards. He always went round the inside and liked to be up there from the start—he was the ideal man for the job.

It was a perfect spring day and the forty-three runners made their usual hair-raising dash for position at the first, where two fell. They soon thinned out and only twenty-four were left standing as they jumped the water at the end of the first circuit with Sheila's Cottage tucked nicely into fifth place behind First of the Dandies, Zahia, Happy Home and Le Daim.

The favourite, Silver Fame, had fallen at Becher's first time and, as usual, the race began to take shape as they crossed Becher's on the second circuit and swung towards the Canal Turn. The winner looked sure to come from one of seven runners—and Sheila's Cottage was among them on the inside. First of the Dandies led over Valentine's and increased his lead as he came onto the racecourse, pursued by Zahia with our horse next, resolutely galloping, just as we knew she would.

Then came the real drama of the race as First of the Dandies jumped the second last just ahead of Zahia. That's where the horses come from the circular course on to the home straight and everyone around me gasped as Zahia continued on the round course and out of the race. By then I could hardly take my eyes off Sheila's Cottage as Arthur drove her relentlessly on in pursuit of First of the Dandies, who jumped the last with a useful looking advantage.

I turned round briefly for a word with the owner and there was John, sitting down, heavily engrossed in a bottle of brandy. 'Look here,' I said, 'we could win the National—aren't you interested?' He just looked up and said,

'You do your job and I'll do mine; you look after the racing and I'll look after the brandy.'

And there was Sheila's Cottage eating up the ground and closing with every stride; she joined the leader 150 yards from the post and though he was tiring and bumped her, she went by him to win by a length.

We'd won the National . . . I could hardly believe it. Everyone was patting me on the back and trying to shake me by the hand—and John, well, I reckon he saw three Sheila's Cottages when he got to the winner's enclosure!

Neville Crump (far left) looks admiringly at Sheila's Cottage in the winner's enclosure after the 1948 Grand National. 'Suddenly I was the wonder boy and everybody wanted me to train for them.'

Back at Warwick House, the pressmen got their picture but jockey Arthur Thompson lost the top of a finger thanks to Sheila's Cottage!

Dear old Sheila's Cottage, she'd done it for me, the first mare to win the National since Shannon Lass in 1902 . . . and after that I never looked back. Suddenly, I was the wonder boy and everyone wanted me to train for them. We soon got full up though they were all jumpers; if I'd had some flat horses I might have had a penny or two now instead of being skint!

We went back to the Adelphi that night and needless to say I didn't get home until the next day when everyone came to Warwick House and gave the horse a fabulous reception. A couple of days later a Press photographer turned up to take her picture with Arthur on top. And what did she do? She bit off the top of one of his fingers while he was trying to put on her bridle! I told him to go to the doctor but he was a tough old sod; he just got up on the horse and they got their picture.

Arthur was a splendid jockey. The nearest we came to a row was at Manchester one day; I was very fond of Manchester, it was a great racecourse. I said to Arthur, 'Now listen, don't go mad on this animal or he won't get the trip; sit in behind and wait.' There were only about four runners. What did he do? He was miles away at the line-up, never got into the race and then came roaring up and just got beat. I was furious and when he got off I said to him, 'Christ almighty, what were you so-and-so well doing?' 'Well,' he said, 'if you think I was that stupid, you'd better ride the next one yourself.' I replied, 'That's a very unkind thing to say, Arthur, you know very well I couldn't.'

Four years later, we were back in the winner's enclosure after the National again, this time with Teal, a horse who no one wanted originally. He was once offered for sale at fifty shillings and later bought, with another horse, for £35. Everyone around Yorkshire seemed to have owned him at one time or another and while Sheila's Cottage was winning her National, Teal was careering round the Yorkshire moors on his own. He was eventually sent to Ridley Lamb of Ingleby, Barwick, and he got him going. He started to win some point-to-points very impressively and was later bought by a Stockton contractor, Harry Lane, for £2,000 in May 1951.

Teal went to the National as 100–7 second favourite to Freebooter, who fell at the Canal Turn second time around. Arthur made a fantastic recovery on Teal after hitting Becher's hard on the second circuit. Teal skidded along on his belly for twenty yards with Arthur calmly sitting there waiting for him to get to his feet. He got him up but down he went again. Arthur stayed in the saddle and Teal then recovered to go on and win by five lengths from Legal Joy ridden by Michael Scudamore.

Arthur put that all down to a good luck charm he had received from his sister in Ireland—a small cross which he put in his breeches and it went round Aintree with him. Funny how little things like that affect you. I've always liked anything with a number three in it. And Sheila's Cottage was number 13 when she won the National!

I've been lucky with my jockeys and Gerry Scott, who rode my third National winner, Merryman II, in 1960, was another brilliant horseman. Mind you, he shouldn't have even ridden in that National. Gerry had a double-fracture of the collar-bone but I persuaded an Irish doctor to let him ride. They'd never have let him go out there in that condition these days.

Arguably, Merryman was my best National winner. He gave a faultless display and won by fifteen lengths at 13–2 from Stan Mellor on Badan-loch—the first favourite to win since Freebooter won in 1950. Merryman would have won it again the following year but was kicked at the start. Derek Ancil rode him and Merryman was still only beaten five lengths by Nicolaus Silver, who was receiving 25 lbs from him. Nicolaus Silver's jockey that day was Bobby Beasley, son-in-law of Arthur Thompson—the very same Arthur Thompson whose skill and dash got Sheila's Cottage home in the National that changed my life.

# MICHAEL DICKINSON

A packet of Trebor mints turned the appropriately named Silver Buck from a kicking, bucking nervous horse into a quiet, lovable cheeky animal who earns pride of place in the Dickinson family for his victory in the Gold Cup at Cheltenham on 18 March 1982 which was, without doubt, the greatest day of my life, for I also trained the second, Bregawn.

Let me emphasise straightaway that we are strictly a family unit and my father Tony did, of course, hold the trainer's licence until the end of the 1979–80 season. While he and I are responsible for most things, we have to bring in Mother when we are stuck on one vote each. We believe in democracy! Mother takes a fantastic interest in the whole operation and works very hard in the yard. She rides out two lots every day and she's the main feeder with the head lad, Brian Powell, who has been with Father a long time. Every day is one long committee meeting; every meal, every five minutes we have together we are discussing one thing or another.

The buying of a horse is Father on conformation and myself on pedigree. And we don't often buy horses with much form as they are too expensive. We bought Silver Buck as a five-year-old from Ireland in April 1977 after he had won two point-to-points and a bumper at Clonmel for the Curragh trainer Paul Doyle. He was a very, very nervous horse. It took us five minutes to catch him in the box to put on the bridle and he spooked at everything. He bucked me off a couple of times so I seldom rode him much at home after that!

He's by Silver Cloud by Aureole, the Queen's horse, who wasn't a particularly good sire, out of a mare by Archive, who was Arkle's sire from a quite good old Irish jumping family. Silver Buck has only an average pedigree, nothing to go overboard about; quite a good-looking horse but he's well made and we reckon he's just about right. Some people say he's too small which isn't so—he's 16.1.

We began training Silver Buck that July but dared not run him until he had quietened down and begun to relax. This meant waiting for the Ambleside Novices Hurdle at Carlisle in November and since it was his first outing, it was decided that I should ride. We only came eighth but at least we finished the course! A month later, my brother-in-law, Thomas Tate, rode him to his first victory in an amateur riders' hurdle at Catterick, and then I won on him at Worcester in a Philip Cornes Novices Hurdle qualifier. I remember arriving home and saying, 'Well, he's won his two hurdle races but that's about all he'll win.' Everyone looked slightly depressed at my remark so I added, 'But he might make quite a good novice chaser next season.'

However, nine days later Silver Buck was out, and winning again, this time at Leicester. We were so pleased, we decided to run in the Bristol Novices Handicap at Haydock where he carried 12st 7 lbs, giving Kelso Chant 29 lbs. Silver Buck was a complete novice still but he gave me just about the best ride I'd ever had on any horse. We just hacked round until going on strongly near the finish to win by one length. It wasn't entirely the fact that we'd won which gave me so much pleasure, but I suddenly felt that we might, just might, have quite a good horse in the yard.

Silver Buck finished his first season by failing to distinguish himself in three more hurdle races and his owner, Jack Mewies, our solicitor, decided to sell and Silver Buck was bought by Mrs Christine Feather who lives close by at Leathley. She agreed that Silver Buck should be put out to grass for the summer and go chasing the following season.

Unfortunately an accident at Cartmel left me with a split liver and ended my riding career so I was never to ride Silver Buck in a race again; it was one of those nasty falls where the horses have no option but to gallop over you. We had to find another jockey, therefore, and decided to engage Tommy Carmody who arrived just in time to start schooling Silver Buck over fences.

Poor Tommy—he was in and out of the saddle in a very short space of time. Silver Buck decided he did not like these new jumps and nothing and no one was going to change his mind so, without much ado, he promptly landed Tommy on the ground and nearly buried him under the wing. I remember standing there and thinking, 'We've got this poor jockey over from Ireland and the third day we damn nearly kill him.' Fortunately, both Tommy and the horse were all right but since then we have a slightly different procedure. Silver Buck and Robert Earnshaw, who looks after him, seem to have a mutual understanding so nowadays Robert does all the schooling and Kevin Whyte the cantering.

Silver Buck is inclined to become bored at home and spends much of his time spooking, peeping, ducking and diving which makes it extremely rough on his jockey and unfortunately he is inclined to continue this behaviour on the course which is why we have always given him two small runs at the start of each season.

All of which brings us back to those Trebor mints; when he first arrived, it was all hell and no idea both in and out of the stable. He bucked and kicked and made it very plain that he preferred to be left alone. His change in character is entirely due to a packet of Trebor mints and the patience and kindness of everyone who handled him during those early days. He would have nothing to do with it when we first offered him a mint, but we left a few in his manger and the following morning they were gone. The same thing happened for quite a few nights and we realised the only time he dared eat them was when everyone had gone home and the yard was quiet. Once having acquired a taste for them, however, he became quite amenable and started taking them from our hands and nowadays he actually comes up looking for a mint! For some reason or other, they've helped make him much more placid and we no longer have the daily wrestling match to put on his bridle, clean his hooves etc. Even the blacksmith uses the same therapy—one Trebor and Silver Buck stands as good as gold!

Silver Buck first wore Mrs Feather's colours in the Greystoke Novices Chase at Teesside on 31 October 1978—and he and Tommy won handsomely by four lengths. He followed up with victories at Stratford and Wetherby where he met that season's subsequent Gold Cup winner, Alverton, for the one and only time and beat him by six lengths in an Embassy Qualifier. Silver Buck went on to win at Leicester but then snow and ice gripped the country and the Embassy Final, scheduled for the end of January, was postponed until 2 March. We could not use our own gallops at Gisburn and therefore had the problem of keeping our horses fit so we boxed them up and took them in relays to Blackpool to work on the beach.

The days went by and the re-arranged Embassy Final drew nearer; we were desperate to give Silver Buck a race. The weather in the south relented and we took him to Windsor just nine days before the Haydock date with Night Nurse. We knew he wasn't fit but just had to give him a run and he raced reasonably well until being brought down by Purdo three from home; as luck would have it, there was no injury to horse or rider, but at least he'd had an outing. Now we just had to sit and wait; we slept, walked and talked of nothing but the Haydock race.

The big day dawned bright and sunny. The ground on the chase course was good which suited both horses and although seven went to post, it looked as if it could be a two-horse race. The punters knew it and made Night Nurse 4–6 favourite and Silver Buck 5–2.

A mile to go and it was between the two; they took each other on and had a tremendous battle over the last seven fences. Ian Watkinson and Night

Nurse came back at Silver Buck and Tommy time and again and neither of these two magnificent animals deserved to be beaten. In the end, it was Night Nurse, the dual Champion Hurdler, who had to be content with second place as Silver Buck came on the stronger to win by two and a half lengths. Our tactics had worked; we had planned to try and outstay Night Nurse and we did just that. Silver Buck is better when he is racing flat out with good horses in good company. We were thrilled; we had beaten an 'unbeatable' horse.

Silver Buck finished his season by going to Cheltenham where once again the going was heavy and he finished third to Master Smudge and Sweet September in the Sun Alliance Novices Chase over three miles.

The 1979–80 season brought further success for Silver Buck at Wincanton and Hereford before he took the Edward Hanmer Memorial Chase at Haydock beating Night Nurse by one and a half lengths; Night Nurse pulled up with an injury to his foreleg which at one time threatened his career. Then we went to Kempton where we really enjoyed the sweet smell of success by winning the King George VI Chase in an eleven-horse field, beating Jack of Trumps and Border Incident with Tied Cottage, the subsequent though eventually disqualified 1980 Gold Cup winner, twenty-seven lengths back in fourth place. Silver Buck won the Compton Chase at Newbury on 9 February 1980 before coming down to earth with a bang at Hereford on 1 March when he struggled home in the Sean Graham Chase by half a length from the comparatively moderate Portway Nick after starting at 6–1 on. He was not himself and we decided not to run in the Gold Cup—in fact he didn't run again that season.

We never did discover exactly what was wrong but we had a fit and healthy Silver Buck in the yard once again for the 1980–81 season, my first holding the trainer's licence. We decided to follow a similar programme with Silver Buck after the previous season's success but since condition or limited races are few and far between, it meant travelling the length and breadth of the country. Fortunately, Mrs Feather was in agreement so we went ahead with the entries.

Silver Buck picked up two small condition races at Worcester and Folkestone before going on to Haydock where he won the Edward Hanmer Memorial Chase for the second year running. His next race should have been at Stockton but bad weather forced the meeting to be cancelled so we had to run him in a handicap at Catterick—the W. L. and Hector Christie Memorial Chase on 13 December, just thirteen days before the King George. He carried 12st 7 lbs in a four-horse field and he does not enjoy racing under those conditions. He made it perfectly obvious from the start what he was going to do—he was going to challenge the lot. Unfortunately two fell in the early stages which left him to gallop against Sunset Cristo, who was 34 lbs better off. It was a hard race, a very hard race, particularly when you consider he was only beaten a length after three gruelling miles.

'That's it,' I thought to myself. 'We've just blown the King George.' How could Silver Buck be expected to take on Anaglogs Daughter, Tied Cottage, Chinrullah, Border Incident, Night Nurse and Diamond Edge, who had just won with 12st at Cheltenham, after a race like that? No way . . .

However, Boxing Day arrived without further incident, until saddling-up time that is. There just didn't seem to be enough pairs of hands; Tommy Stack was helping to saddle, Mrs Feather was fetching bucket and sponge and everyone else was dashing to and fro trying to be helpful. We'd just got nicely saddled when a steward walked by and said, 'When you're ready, Mr Dickinson.' We thought we'd made it until Tommy quietly remarked, 'Well, everything's fine but where's the number cloth?'

I can assure you that this is not the sort of procedure I recommend before any race, let alone a big one! By that time, I was concerned only with getting to the start and, if we managed that, I'd be delighted to finish fourth. The punters did not share my view for they made Silver Buck the 9–4 favourite to win the race for the second successive year.

At last they were off, a select band of eight and, as expected the Irish mare Anaglogs Daughter went ahead at a million miles an hour; at one stage she was almost a fence clear. This left Tommy Carmody in a very difficult position. He doubted whether Anaglogs Daughter would make the three miles but she is a good horse and he dared not take the risk of allowing her twenty lengths clear so, with a mile to go, he started the chase. He took her on four out and luckily the mare did exactly as Tommy wanted. She refused to give in and each time Silver Buck appeared to have the edge, back she came again. That is just the kind of race Silver Buck most enjoys.

Tommy knew he had left Night Nurse quite a way behind but also knew the challenge would still come—and it did. The crowd started to roar in anticipation as Night Nurse closed the gap; would they see a repeat of that dramatic set to at Haydock twenty-one months before? Unfortunately, Alan Brown might have covered the ground just a little too fast for Night Nurse made two bad mistakes, the first three out when Alan made a miraculous recovery to stay in the saddle, but he had no chance of staying aboard at the last as Night Nurse ploughed through the fence leaving Silver Buck and Tommy, who had jumped impeccably throughout, to race away and win by five lengths from Anaglogs Daughter with Diamond Edge a further five lengths back in third.

There are still some people who think that Night Nurse would have won but for faltering; the fact remains he did, and Silver Buck didn't and jumping's the name of the game. There's no doubt in my mind that Silver Buck was the best 3-mile chaser in the country on the day and fifteen months later he won the supreme accolade by triumphing in the Gold Cup at Cheltenham.

Yet a thousand and one things seemed to go wrong in between, not least of all his performance in the 1981 Gold Cup when he finished third behind Little Owl and Night Nurse. Several of our horses ran badly at Cheltenham that year—Rathgorman, Badsworth Boy and Silver Buck all came down the hill and then absolutely stopped as though they had been shot. With Silver Buck, it was slightly different because people kept bombarding me with the view that the horse would not stay the 3¼ miles of the Gold Cup—I was about the only person on Cheltenham racecourse that day who remained convinced he would.

I never had any doubt that he was a stayer and when we got him home and blood was down his nose from a broken blood vessel, I almost felt a sense of relief; a broken blood vessel is a very effective way of stopping a horse! On top of which he undoubtedly had a touch of the virus along with several other horses in the yard.

Undaunted, therefore, we set out on the road to Cheltenham once again. Silver Buck recovered from his troubles in the summer and we took him to Wincanton for the Terry Biddlecombe Challenge Trophy Chase on 29 October. He started at 6–1 on in a field of three and won by a couple of lengths from Brother Will. Tommy Carmody had returned to Ireland at the end of the 1980–81 season and I decided to stick with my young jockeys in the yard for the new season and that was the first time Robert Earnshaw had ridden Silver Buck in a race. I had every confidence in him. He was still Silver Buck's lad and had, of course, become very attached to the horse and I knew he would ride him well.

But Robert's world—and mine—seemed to crash around him in Silver Buck's next race, the 3-mile Rehearsal Chase at Chepstow on 7 November. There were only four runners and Silver Buck started 3–1 on this time, but he was never jumping well. With hindsight, Robert should have pulled him up but that's easier said than done when you're on a long odds-on shot and Silver Buck had begun to weaken dramatically when he fell at the fourth last. He was completely exhausted and his running was too bad to be true; he was still very poorly when we got him back to Yorkshire.

All I could do was leave Silver Buck in the capable hands of George Foster, who looks after all the sick horses in the yard. We never really discovered what the trouble was but George worked his magic, knowing that I was very keen to run Silver Buck if at all possible in the Edward Hanmer Memorial Handicap Chase at Haydock on 25 November which he

Silver Buck takes the final fence in the 1982 Cheltenham Gold Cup with stable companion Bregawn on the right

had won the previous two years. Silver Buck loves Haydock but, even so, it was a big decision whether to run him or not. We decided to go for it but I was petrified before the race. I felt my head was on the block. If something had gone wrong, if the horse had run another listless race, people would have said, 'You don't deserve to have a good horse.' It was the toughest decision of my life.

Everything turned out fine. Young Robert Earnshaw could not take the ride as he might have been required for Wayward Lad in the King George and we wanted John Francome to ride Silver Buck in a race beforehand.

John gave him a lovely ride, taking it up three from home and going on to win by 1½ lengths from Sunset Cristo, who was to be third at Cheltenham the following March. John was full of praise for Silver Buck after the race and left me in no doubt that he would love the ride again. He said Silver Buck gave him a super ride until he hit the front and then he needed ten men to hold him!

We were once more on Cloud Nine—and soon off it again. The King George was one of the many races to fall victim of the appalling weather but the scheduled day of the race, Boxing Day, brought our next nightmare.

Brian Powell, found Silver Buck lame in his box when he went in with the early morning feed; he could not put his off-hind to the ground. At first we thought it was a bruise but after a couple of days it was obvious it was not, so we had it X-rayed. That revealed no broken bones but he was still lame and remained in his box for a month.

The Gold Cup seemed an impossible dream and I almost resigned myself to missing Cheltenham, but by the beginning of February he was out walking and then on 13 February he did his first canter. George Foster had done a marvellous job with the horse; he went out through the snow and ice every night to treat him and my vet, Anthony Stirk, was tremendous, too. Together, they had nursed the horse back to health. But could we get him fit enough to tackle the cracks at Cheltenham?

In the meantime, the previous year's winner, Little Owl, had been withdrawn from the race and his stable companion Night Nurse installed as ante-post favourite. Silver Buck had only once ever finished behind Night Nurse—at Cheltenham in 1981 when he definitely wasn't right. I felt sure he could win if we could get Silver Buck there. But there was no way we could go to Cheltenham without getting a race into him and I decided to go for the Cox Moore (Sweaters) Handicap Chase over 3-miles at Market Rasen on 6 March, just twelve days before the Gold Cup. I worked the horse hard, so hard in fact that he could easily have reacted badly; and, indicated 'You're giving me too much work, sod this,' and packed it in! But he was terrific and did everything I asked him.

Silver Buck did two splendid gallops each over a mile before Market Rasen with Kevin Whyte, as usual, riding him. Kevin's a very, very good work-rider and Silver Buck goes well for him—and he went well for him at Market Rasen, too, where he jumped superbly and won by one and a half lengths. Robert Earnshaw went to Haydock that day to ride Bregawn in the Greenall Whitley Breweries Handicap Chase so I was delighted that Kevin should have had a piece of the action.

Lady Luck at last seemed on our side. Silver Buck came home and ate up well and his blood figures were the best for four years. I planned his last serious gallop the Saturday before Cheltenham when he went a mile with Rathgorman. He could not have pleased me more. At home, he'll usually cruise along with a couple of furlongs to go, then drop his bit and we never know whether he's gone badly, isn't feeling too well or whether he's being lazy. He makes it very difficult for us to understand what's going on in his mind. But it was different this time. He really worked well, finished in front of Rathgorman who had won five races in a row, and looked like a fighting cock. I gave him just one more spin over two furlongs two days before Cheltenham to blow him out, then boxed him up and sent him on his way on the Wednesday.

By then, I confess, things had changed again; thirteen hours of non-stop rain had put the meeting in jeopardy and one thing was certain, the going would be heavy—the very thing we did not want. I always knew we'd never get the ground we wanted at Cheltenham but this was too bad to be true after all the troubles of the previous months. I felt drained—until the Wednesday, the middle day of the meeting, when Rathgorman stormed away to win the Queen Elizabeth The Queen Mother Two-Mile Champion Chase. That gave me real hope for he went through the going with no trouble and, of course, they use a new course for the Thursday racing, so much of the ground would not be poached.

Silver Buck had travelled down perfectly together with Bregawn, who we decided should also take his chance in the field of twenty-two, the biggest ever for the Gold Cup. Gary Williams, our new travelling head lad, walked him round and Graham Rennison who had always led up Silver Buck and looked after him so well when he went away in previous seasons, had charge of Bregawn. And me? Well, I decided not to struggle through the crowds to find a place in the stands; I sat down in front of the television in the Stewards' hospitality room attached to the weighing room.

What a race! I'll never forget it for the rest of my life. Old Tied Cottage took them along at a cracking gallop and did not surrender the lead until the fourth last, the fence at the top of the hill, where Sunset Cristo took over. But the fourteen-year-old battled back and was in front again three out, only to give way to Silver Buck. Had Robert hit the front too soon? My heart was pounding but Robert had read the situation correctly and, as he approached the last, there was only one danger—Bregawn. Graham Bradley, another of my fine young riders, had brought him along perfectly but this was Silver Buck's day and he was always going that bit better. There were two lengths between them at the line; typical Silver Buck, he never wins by more than is necessary! And immediately after the finish, both jockeys had their arms round each other, patting each other's horse—a gesture which demonstrated the team spirit we have at Harewood.

A moment to treasure for Michael Dickinson and his jockey Robert Earnshaw after the Queen Mother had presented the Cheltenham Gold Cup

That victory—my third from four runners at the Festival—took my prize money for the season to £266,785 enabling me to pass Peter Easterby's record £234,000 of the previous season but there are so many people who have shared in my success and I am grateful to them all, not least my mother and father, and the staff at Harewood who all work and pull together to make a fine team.

And Silver Buck? He is very much a modern-day chaser, the old-fashioned type is not a lot of use these days. They've no speed and take too long to come to themselves and then tend to be heavy-topped with leg and wind problems. The fences are a little softer than they used to be so we don't need such tank-like animals. What we need today is a speedy type like Silver Buck, a magnificent chaser. He has changed so much and matured tremendously since he came to us; it is phenomenal how he improved in the 1981–82 season at the age of ten. Certainly, he seems much happier at Harewood than he was at Gisburn and actually appears to enjoy the all-weather gallop which gives him the good going he appreciates most . . . although don't forget the going was heavy on that marvellous day at Cheltenham, 18 March 1982!

# JOHN DUNLOP

The English-Irish Derby double by Shirley Heights made 1978 a memorable year for me, twelve years after taking out a full trainer's licence. At that time, he was only the fifth horse to win both races, but it was the Irish triumph which was particularly satisfying for the whole saga put a few years on me and added some grey hairs!

The Derby itself is a terribly hard race to win whatever happens and one would always be delighted to be in the first four; but having won at Epsom, we were expected to follow up in Ireland—indeed, I expected to win easily. In the end, it was an even more worrying and shattering experience and such a relief when Shirley Heights was finally given the verdict at The Curragh on 1 July 1978.

Two years earlier, I had been excited at the prospect of training the Mill Reef colt out of Hardiemma, whose reputation preceded him on the journey from Garrowby in Yorkshire to my Arundel stables in Sussex. Apparently, he was rough and a bit of a bully in the paddock and had been turned out with some cattle rather than kept with any of his contemporaries.

He wasn't a particularly fine individual when he arrived in September 1976; not very big, a solid, rather fat horse but with a lot of character. He always showed great independence and strength, both physical and mental. He was a lovely rich mahogany bay, with no white on him at all, just a small star.

Shirley Heights was in many ways an infuriating horse throughout his career and right from the start he did as little as possible at home. He was a very stuffy horse and a lazy worker. He carried a lot of condition and showed very little speed. Finally, we thought we'd better give him a run which might prove something.

We chose the 6-furlong Teesside Caravan Stakes on 10 June 1977 for his debut, primarily because it was at York, the local course of his owners, the late Lord Halifax and his son, Lord Irwin. He ran rather drearily, never getting into the race at any stage and finishing fifth, beaten eight and a half lengths, but it had at least given him a race and we felt it must have done him some good. Despite this, he didn't appear to have shed much condition or show any more enthusiasm working after the York race.

However, we ran him two weeks later in the Margaret Maiden Stakes at Doncaster, again over 6 furlongs. Ron Hutchinson rode him again and he should have won, but was interfered with and he finished well in second place behind a Bruce Hobbs horse, Cunard. That was a great step up from his debut but even so it wasn't a particularly good performance by what was hopefully, potentially, a first class horse.

He ran next on 7 July at Newmarket in the Limekilns Stakes over 7 furlongs and he was really impressive, winning by a short head from Sexton Blake; he came from some way behind and really stuck his head out, battling all the way and finishing well. The encouraging thing was the way he won; for the first time I thought this was, after all, probably going to be a good horse.

We decided to raise him in grade and sent him north again on 9 August for Newcastle's Seaton Delaval Stakes over 7 furlongs but the ground turned out rock hard and he didn't like it at all, finishing third behind Sexton Blake and Labienus. We certainly blamed the going for that defeat though it was a falsely run race and he didn't get into it at all. A couple of weeks later, he injured a front leg when rolling in his box; not a severe injury but enough to prevent him working for about a fortnight.

We wanted to run him in Sandown's Intercraft Solario Stakes, again over 7 furlongs; it looked an ideal race for him. This hold up almost ruled that out although he responded quickly to treatment. We hadn't been able to do a great deal with him before the Sandown race on 2 September and, to make matters worse, it poured and poured the night before and on the morning of the race, the going was very soft. We were in two minds whether to run him but in the end Shirley Heights took his chance and actually ran a marvellous race. He was a bit unlucky not to win, after being checked in the final furlong as he was making his run. He lost his momentum and, because he was short of a gallop, naturally weakened and couldn't quicken again, eventually being beaten a couple of lengths by Peter Walwyn's subsequently disappointing horse, Bolak.

Touch wood, his leg was perfectly all right after that and he had his final race as a two-year-old in Ascot's Royal Lodge Stakes over 1 mile on 24 September. Although he wandered a furlong out, he won well enough by three-quarters of a length. I wasn't there as I'd gone to Ireland to see North Stoke run—and win, as it turned out, the Joe McGrath Memorial Stakes. Ron Hutchinson, my stable jockey, had the choice between riding North

Stoke in Ireland or Shirley Heights at Ascot; he chose North Stoke so the Halifaxes asked for Greville Starkey as he had ridden for them regularly when their horses were trained at Newmarket by John Oxley. Hutch sadly retired that autumn and so Greville actually rode Shirley Heights in all his races as a three-year-old.

My vet and I decided it might be beneficial to give Shirley Heights' front legs a light blister because of the injury he had prior to the Royal Lodge; it had left a bit of a callous on the tendon and so we let him down and blistered him which meant he had to stand in his box doing nothing from November to mid-January. Surprisingly enough, considering he was such a ruffian of a horse, he behaved beautifully and developed very well physically. Some horses will lose their condition, all their muscle; he didn't.

Then we started him off again in February, trotting first of all and then cantering but it was terribly wet throughout March and April and we had an awful job getting him fit. He was so idle; it was impossible to get him to do as much as I wanted.

I decided to give him some variety and Guy Harwood very kindly let me take him to Pulborough and work there with Man of Harlech—who the Halifaxes had bought from Lavinia, Duchess of Norfolk—who led Shirley Heights in his work as a three-year-old. I was given permission to work him after racing at Newbury. Man of Harlech had a minor injury at the time so I took Traquair, another grand old servant of mine, with Shirley Heights and, looking back, that really was rather amusing. Traquair was a marvellous horse at home, a great lead horse; he bowled off in front, Greville Starkey and the so-called Classic horse couldn't get anywhere near him. Shirley Heights blew hard afterwards but I believe Greville told one or two pals that he didn't think much of the whole business!

I wasn't particularly surprised when he finished ten lengths behind Whitstead first time out as a three-year-old in the $1\frac{1}{4}$-mile Classic Trial Stakes at Sandown on 22 April because he certainly needed the race. He then won the Heathorn Stakes at Newmarket on 4 May narrowly but impressively enough giving 10 lbs to Ile de Bourbon and went on to take the Mecca-Dante Stakes at York on 17 May in really smashing style. I asked Greville after that race whether he thought he'd act at Epsom and Greville replied, 'It doesn't matter whether he acts or not, he'll still win!'

And win he did on 7 June coming from a long way back at the bottom of the hill and getting up to win by a head from Hawaiian Sound to achieve for me the ambition of every trainer in winning the Derby. I felt very strongly that he was a natural to go on to The Curragh and hopefully win the Irish Sweeps Derby twenty-four days later. There was no danger that I was doing too much with him; indeed, with hindsight, I think he was a horse who

should have been kept racing all year win or lose. He had a fantastic constitution and was so solid and tough, but only prepared to exert himself on the racecourse.

However, Lord Halifax and his wife had very strong traditional feelings that a serious Classic horse and, in this case a Derby winner, should be given a break after Epsom and let down before being trained for the St Leger; they were very determined and adamant that Shirley Heights was not going to Ireland.

We started working on them in a quiet but persuasive way and I rallied as

Shirley Heights and his regular work rider, Rodney Boult, under the watchful eye of John Dunlop at Arundel many friends as I could to my cause. Lavinia, Duchess of Norfolk, was particularly helpful and Major Victor McCalmont said he'd ask them over to Ireland for the weekend and that might be the added encouragement they needed. I strongly wanted to go to Ireland for I felt The Curragh would suit Shirley Heights better than Epsom, the field looked weaker and one hoped he would win and still have a fairly easy race. To me, it was an obvious progression from Epsom. The Halifaxes finally agreed, so Shirley Heights and I were able to get back to work!

He obviously didn't do much in the first week after the Derby and I planned three bits of work over seven furlongs just to keep the edge on him; however, he was more lazy than ever and not at all impressive in his gallops. Even so, I wasn't particularly worried as he'd had three races before the Derby and was a fit horse.

Man of Harlech went with him to Ireland on the Thursday before the race in order to gallop together on the racecourse the following morning. He travelled over well and, for the piece of work, I chose a five-furlong stretch they call the Flat Rath which is quite a steep, climbing gallop right up the middle of The Curragh, but running left to right parallel to the finishing straight. Shirley Heights was full of himself and very much on his toes, behaving quite stupidly. His usual work rider, Rodney Boult, rode him and Shirley Heights' lad, Malcolm Gould, was on Man of Harlech. However, Shirley Heights worked beautifully, much, much more freely and strongly than he'd been doing at home; I suppose the change of environment had sharpened him up and given him a bit of interest.

But when I got up to him just after they pulled up, Shirley Heights was blowing and heaving like an old grampus; I'd never known the horse blow like this before. Of course, I'd given him a week to get over the Derby and he'd been relatively lazy in those three bits of work at home and I hadn't been particularly worried, but I should have been. Obviously he'd done even less than I thought. He was a very, very gross feeder and ate anything that was put in front of him; clearly he'd got himself remarkably unfit in a very short period. It was too late to do anything about it then but I consoled myself that he'd done a good bit of work. I still wasn't all that perturbed.

Lord and Lady Halifax came over for the race with their son and daughter-in-law, Lord Irwin and Lady Irwin. I have to admit even now that Lady Halifax, particularly, was still dubious about the wisdom of bringing the horse to Ireland. Anyway, we were there and I went with Lord and Lady Irwin to a rather rickety stand they have for photographers which is just past the winning post and looking straight down the racecourse; in retrospect, it was an extremely bad place to see what was happening at the finishing line.

Hawaiian Sound set a cracking pace and Shirley Heights got a little far behind turning into the straight. Both Shirley Heights and Exdirectory edged out towards the middle of the course as Hawaiian Sound stayed on the rail, or nearside rail to us from our rickety stand, and they finished spread right across the course almost in a line. I had no idea whether we'd won or not; in fact, I was inclined to think we were beaten and Peter Irwin shared my pessimism. We discussed it briefly before going down to meet Greville and I remember saying, 'Oh, my God, that's the one thing we didn't want to happen; he's had a hard race and been beaten.' Everything seemed to have gone wrong and it looked as if we should have followed the route Peter's parents preferred.

It seemed ages before the result was announced—then, relief, Shirley Heights first by a head from Exdirectory with Hawaiian Sound a neck away third and Inkerman fourth a length further back. Not the way I'd expected our 5–4 favourite to win, but at least he'd done it. We learned afterwards that Greville had suffered with cramp from about the halfway point of the

Shirley Heights (second right) just gets the better of Exdirectory in the 1978 Irish Derby at the Curragh race and hadn't been able to give the horse as much encouragement as he'd have wished, so there was an awful lot of drama one way or another and I've never been so relieved to hear a verdict. Even then, many people felt we had interfered with Exdirectory and they were certainly close together at one stage, but I'd had enough drama for one day!

Shirley Heights, alas, never ran again: I'd just started to get him back into work and had received permission to gallop him at Goodwood at the beginning of August, again for a change of scenery since he'd been as lazy as ever at Arundel! He danced and jumped about before he went out on to the racecourse and at one stage slipped and skidded without actually falling. He regained his feet and went off and did his work, and he did it quite well though he sweated a lot and blew hard afterwards. I'd never seen him sweat as much even after a race and that night we found he'd injured a leg, not a severe injury but enough to stop him racing again. He retired to the Sandringham Stud in 1979.

# PETER EASTERBY

The victory of Alverton in the 1979 Gold Cup at the Cheltenham Festival is the race which really gave me the most tremendous pleasure. When a brave horse has broken down very badly on both forelegs, been fired, and off the course for more than a year and a half and then comes back to win a great race, it is an occasion one never forgets.

I had bought Alverton's dam, Alvertona, a chestnut filly, as a yearling for one of my owners, Mr Bill Pratt of Northallerton, and she had won a couple of races as a two-year-old for him. I also had Alverton's half-sister Tinella and won with her while I had Alverton throughout his racing days. When you have known a family for fifteen years, they seem to become part of you and that, added to Alverton's comeback after being fired, did make his Cheltenham Gold Cup something special.

Alverton was a good bright chestnut, standing about 16.2, a typical jumping type but not with the quality of a horse like Sea Pigeon. Alverton was a longish horse, with plenty of bone, a pronounced jumping bump and, most important of all, full of guts; I suppose you could describe him as a tough, plain horse.

He was a very good doer and I think I can sum him up by saying that he needed plenty of work and plenty to eat—that was Alverton; I have a 1¼-mile all-weather strip at Habton which I use a lot in hard and wet weather, and when I want to school my jumpers I take them up to work on the Malton gallops on Langton Wold, five miles away; my ordinary grass gallops are at Habton near the all-weather strip.

Alverton was a very relaxed horse but funnily enough his dam Alvertona was highly strung and just the opposite. Sweat used to run off her and Alverton's half-sister Tinella used to sweat, too. She had more quality than Alverton and was quite a decent filly but was finished by the virus.

Mr Pratt decided to keep Alvertona for his stud and I arranged for her to be mated in 1969 with Mr Paul Mellon's Cambridgeshire winner Mid-summer Night II. The resulting colt foal was Alverton who was big and backward as a two-year-old and was cut. I bought him as a potential dual-purpose horse towards the end of his two-year-old days, and when he began to show promise six months later, passed him on to Mr Stanhope Joel for whom I had already trained useful jumping winners in Pandolfi and Chamos. Mr Joel had not had Alverton long before he won a maiden plate for him at Haydock in August 1973, another at Newcastle over 1½ miles a fortnight later, and he really pleased me at the Western Meeting at Ayr when, in spite of a rough passage, he won a good 10-furlong handicap.

The Joel family were delighted and, six weeks after Ayr, he won a novice hurdle in a trot at Newcastle. He won again at Wetherby in heavy ground at the beginning of February and a fortnight later we took him to Newcastle again for a four-year-old hurdle but he broke down when cantering and was pulled up two out. I have never understood what happened. It came out of the blue. There was nothing to do but ask the Joels to be patient, fire him and give him eighteen months on the sidelines, which they readily agreed to. It was disappointing, but we felt Alverton had a real future as a jumper if he would stand training.

In November 1975, I took Alverton, now a five-year-old and sound again, to Newcastle to win a handicap hurdle. He won another hurdle at Uttoxeter in March, and then went back to the Flat and showed his guts, determination and will-to-succeed by winning five handicaps off the reel, finishing second in the Ebor at York to Sir Montagu and winning two more handicaps in September. He had had a marvellous year on the Flat but, as a hurdler in the first half of the 1977–78 season, he got too high in the handicap after winning at Doncaster first time out, just missed the bus and we decided to turn to chasing.

With hindsight, it was definitely the right decision. His first race over fences was at Newcastle in the middle of January 1978. Sweet Joe, the odds-on favourite, and Alverton drew right away from the rest of the field, which included a couple of other useful novices. Alverton came from behind to tackle Sweet Joe, jumped the last the better and held on well on the flat to get home by three-quarters of a length. Two months later, they were both to win at the National Hunt Meeting at Cheltenham.

We took Alverton to Newbury at the beginning of March to tackle Sweet Joe again in the Sam Cowan Novice Chase. Since Newcastle, Sweet Joe had been very impressive when winning the Nottingham Champion Novices' Chase and was fully expected to turn the tables on us but, in fact, we won at Newbury much more easily than we had at Newcastle—by twenty lengths.

Ten days later, Sweet Joe went to Cheltenham and won the Sun Alliance

Chase on the first day of the National Hunt Meeting. Alverton's race was the Arkle Challenge Trophy on the second day of the meeting. He was to have been ridden by Jonjo O'Neill but Jonjo was hurt on the first day, and Graham Thorner took his place. The Arkle Challenge Trophy was, as expected, a highly competitive race with ten winners of novice chases in the field, and the Irishman Straight Row a hot favourite. Alverton barely made a mistake, showed himself a really brave horse, and won on merit. We decided to give him a long rest and wait for the new jumping season.

Alverton began what was to prove his last season by running second over 2½ miles at Wetherby. Then he was brought down in the Massey Ferguson Gold Cup at Cheltenham when going well, before being beaten on Boxing Day in a 2-mile chase at Wetherby, which was too sharp for him. Five weeks later at Sandown he just failed to give 3 lbs to the future Whitbread Gold Cup and Hennessy winner, Diamond Edge. Possibly, Alverton just needed the race; he had every chance and looked like winning but Diamond Edge beat him by half a length.

Alverton takes the final fence in the 1979 Cheltenham Gold Cup just behind Tied Cottage as the snow tumbles down

As Alverton thrived on racing, I felt sure the Sandown race would bring him on and a month later we took him to Haydock for the Greenall Whitley Breweries Handicap Chase. I thought he would improve on his Sandown form, and this he did, for he won easily from Rambling Artist, who had won the race the previous year, and the Grand National winner, Lucius. Prior to Haydock, our long-term objective with Alverton had been the Grand National, but we had also entered him in the Cheltenham Gold Cup, and, after the race, I said to Mr Joel's daughter, Mrs Brudenell-Bruce: 'What shall we do now? Shall we go first for the Cheltenham Gold Cup?' She and her sister said yes, definitely, and were clearly very keen to do so. Alverton had finished first or second in eight of his nine steeplechases and been brought down in the ninth. It was a record which entitled him to go for the Gold Cup.

I took half a dozen horses to Cheltenham for the 1979 National Hunt Meeting but things did not go well for the stable to start with. On the Tuesday, Little Owl was just beaten by Willie Wumpkins in the long-distance hurdle and Promiment King was brought down in the Sun Alliance Chase, while Sea Pigeon, Within The Law and Major Thompson finished second, fourth and seventh to Monksfield in the Waterford Crystal Champion Hurdle the following day. As the Thursday dawned the weather was deteriorating with snow on the way.

We decided to run both my Champion hurdler Night Nurse and Alverton, who Jonjo chose to ride, in the Gold Cup. Alverton and the previous year's runner-up, Brown Lad, were joint favourites in the field of fourteen with Night Nurse and Gaffer joint second favourites and the New Zealand-bred Royal Mail and Tied Cottage among others fancied. A heavy flurry of snow made conditions unpleasant but Tied Cottage, as usual, tried to lead from pillar to post and had most of the field off the bit at the bottom end of the course second time round. Two fences from the finish, Alverton was closing with Tied Cottage and was perhaps three lengths behind and as they came to the last the race lay between them, and I thought Tied Cottage definitely showed signs of beginning to tire. The Irish horse changed his legs approaching the last and the two took off almost together but Tied Cottage collapsed on landing, leaving Alverton to finish on his own. He had jumped round almost perfectly and was so game and brave that I felt certain in my own mind that he would have worn Tied Cottage down, if the latter had not fallen.

It was a marvellous moment and when I returned home and looked up Alverton's record, I found that it was his twenty-fifth race under National Hunt rules and that he had won eleven of them and had never been out of the first three in his ten races over fences except when he was brought down.

Gold Cup smiles
from jockey Jonjo
O'Neill and Peter
Easterby in the
winner's enclosure
with Alverton

In addition, he had won eleven races on the Flat—the record of a very courageous horse.

What next? It was decided that we should stick to our original plan with Alverton and go for the Grand National on 31 March in which, on his Gold Cup form, he was chucked into the handicap with only 10 st 13 lbs—about a stone less than he was entitled to carry after Cheltenham. On the eve of the National, the stable brought off an Aintree hat-trick with Night Nurse in a 2-mile chase, Major Thompson in a 2-mile hurdle and Anna's Prince in the Red Rum Novices' Handicap Chase. The stable was in form, the going was good on the Grand National course, Alverton appeared none the worse for Cheltenham and naturally he was a hot favourite.

There were thirty-four runners and at halfway, after jumping the water, Alverton lay fourth, going well and, as far as I could see, jumping brilliantly. I was full of hope as they went away from the stands for the second time but he hit the fence after the first open ditch hard, brushed through the next and barely rose at all at Becher's, fell on his neck and was apparently killed instantly.

Mrs Brudenell-Bruce, after seeing the film of the race, thought that there was something wrong with Alverton as he approached Becher's and that he might well have had a heart attack in mid-air. We shall never know. It was a ghastly moment for us all, a brave horse had suddenly gone, as may always happen in jumping. I shall not forget that day at Aintree, but I shall always remember much more vividly Alverton's twenty-second victory—his great triumph in the 1979 Cheltenham Gold Cup.

# TIM FORSTER

A horse with legs as bad as it was possible to have and with lung and asthmatic trouble somehow defied everything and triumphed against all the odds to win a 2½-mile chase over those difficult Sandown fences for an unbelievable victory at the Military Meeting on 10 March 1979.

He had been a lunatic of an animal, the laughing stock of the yard, yet that day at Sandown in only his third race in three years, three nightmare years, he showed the courage I saw in him when I first spotted him as a big, lanky, overgrown three-year-old with a very ugly head at the Doncaster Sales in May 1973. For all that, I liked him then—and six years later, he made me so very proud.

I went to have another look at him when he was led out unsold from the ring but I was not the only one to have fallen for this ugly duckling. In his box, I found David Smyly, now a Racecourse Judge, who was also hoping to buy him privately. It seemed stupid for us to bid against each other and we decided that one of us would try and buy him and we would go half shares. The vendor was an Irish lady and the deal took more than a little time, but finally he was ours.

I had few, if any, of the misgivings I usually have after I've made a purchase as this horse had a certain charm, if that is the right word. He looked ugly, common and wild, but also very courageous. However, my faith in my purchase was slightly shattered when a very well-known Irish trainer, humorist and a noted Sales attender, came towards me. 'Have you just bought that No Argument three-year-old?' 'Yes,' I said, 'I have.' 'You have gone down in my estimation. How could you buy a horse that looks like that?' he said. 'However ugly your wife was, it would be better to stay in bed with her than get up in the morning and look at that fellow!'

The horse was broken in and proved more than a handful and after a few months came into training with me. He was wild, he sweated up every day, he ran away, he was almost untrainable. However, work began to cure

Tim Forster at home
at Letcombe Bassett

some of the evils and, with the skill of my head lad, John Humphreys, and Ken Dorsett, the lad who looked after him, it soon became obvious that he could go a bit. Nobody wanted to ride him in the mornings; he became a joke, and there was a dread for anybody whose name was down to ride him, so it had to be John or Ken and they manfully accepted the task.

If he was going to run, he needed a name and one evening a flash of brilliance—at least I thought so—came to me; by No Argument out of Love Apple—Forbidden Fruit seemed to fit perfectly. Thus he was named. His first race was eventually at Ludlow in Divison Three, Part One of the suitably named Bull Ring Juvenile Novices' Hurdle on 1 March 1974 and David Smyly and I set off in fear and trepidation. It poured with rain. Would he go mad in the paddock? Would he run out? Would he fail to jump? Would he get round those tight bends? He still looked unbelievably backward and a great, gawky baby, yet he skated up, winning by ten lengths. It was too good to be true. We couldn't get over the fact that he was able to win first time out.

This horse had always looked from the day we bought him as if he would need time and be six or seven before he won but if they can go, they seem to be able to go right from the start. We decided not to run him again that season but to give him more time, so out to grass he went.

Sadly, David Smyly had to sell his share during the summer as he had then become a licensed judge and was therefore no longer allowed to own a racehorse. We sold out to Lord Michael Pratt and Graham Cooper and his father, who were all friends of David's. When The Fruit, as he was then known to everyone, came up from grass, he was still wild or, to be precise, a lunatic, despite great efforts by Patricia Smyly to be nice to him during his holiday with her.

He ran well in the 1974–75 season and won again over hurdles at Warwick but we still felt he needed more time and we would not hurry him.

He won the twenty-runner Marksman Handicap Hurdle by five lengths at Chepstow first time out the following season and, though he was still wild at home, he was getting better with each day and we had begun to understand him and become rather fond of his eccentricity. Then disaster struck at Huntingdon on 9 March 1976 when The Fruit, after making all the running in the 3-mile Ward Hill Handicap Hurdle, faltered as he came to the last, was passed on the run-in and finished second to Jan Stewer. He was so lame, he could hardly walk back to the unsaddling enclosure and we very nearly didn't get him home that night. He had put his foot in a hole and had broken down very, very badly on the near-fore. He was bandaged and poulticed but the leg was enormous; his tendon was shattered and things looked bad. So bad in fact that I told the owners I thought we would have to put him down as he would certainly never race again.

I sent for the veterinary surgeon, Mr Geoffrey Brain, a few days later to come and make a decision whether there was any future for the horse as a racehorse, or anything else for that matter. Mr Brain looked at the leg and shook his head. He felt the leg and shook his head again before finally asking: 'Is he any good?' 'Yes,' I replied. 'Then in that case we will try and save him but I don't hold out much hope. If he is only moderate, it is not worth trying, but if you want to have a go, then we will.' I said, 'Let's have a go.' Mr Brain put the leg in plaster to give the horse some support and when he was sound enough to travel, The Fruit returned, still in plaster, to his devoted friend and nurse Patricia Smyly at Broadway.

Time is a great healer and as the months passed and the plaster had been removed, The Fruit became sound again and, finally after eighteen months' convalescence, he was returned to Letcombe Bassett to see if he could start training. His leg looked and felt horrible and one feared, as each day passed, the next day could be the last.

Gradually, however, he became fitter and after weeks and weeks of roadwork and cantering, he was ready for faster work and even more frighteningly, a school for we had decided that we would run him over fences, hoping that the slightly slower pace than hurdle races would give him a better chance. He schooled brilliantly from the start and, as his work was speeded up, it appeared that much of his old ability was still there. However, another affliction reared its ugly head in the shape of a cough which turned to asthma and once again his programme was interrupted. He seemed a sick horse and was hardly able to breathe.

We eventually returned to the racecourse twenty-five months after his Huntingdon horror and ran in the Betterton Chase at Newbury on 8 April 1978. He ran and jumped well and what's more, to the amazement of all concerned, he was sound after the race. He ran, albeit badly, just once more that season, at Warwick in April and, after the race, was found to be coughing and off-colour. So it was grass again with the leg in reasonably good shape but his lungs apparently on the decline. We decided that only a very long rest would help put matters right, if indeed his wind would ever recover sufficiently for him to be any good as a racehorse.

The following autumn, he came up later than usual from Patricia Smyly who had bedded him on shavings, turned him out in the fresh air every day, damped his hay and other food and slowly started to give him some work. When he returned to Letcombe Bassett this time, it was not only the still horrible looking leg that was worrying, but also his wind. Slowly but surely The Fruit got fitter but it was near winter by now and he had always preferred good going and there wasn't too much of that about. We also knew that heavy going would over-tax his wind and legs so we just had to sit and wait and hope for a dry time. Happily, it came with the March winds and it was decided that The Fruit should run at Sandown in the 2½-mile Beech Open Novices' Chase at the Military meeting.

The horse seemed very fit but he hadn't run for ten months and so whether he was fit enough to win had to be taken on trust. He was declared to run at 10 a.m. on 9 March with the Sandown going forecast as good. The heavens opened at 11 a.m. and it continued to pour with rain for nearly twenty-four hours. As I left the course at Sandown on the Friday evening, I decided The Fruit could not possibly run.

I feared he might not be fit enough for a race on a course which resembled a ploughed field and anyhow his legs and lungs were in no way capable of standing up to the strain. I tried to contact the owners on the Saturday morning to ask permission to withdraw the horse but I was unable to reach them as they were on their way, by train, from Doncaster. I eventually found them at the course and explained my predicament which they fully understood. However, after much deliberation, they decided that it was now or never—The Fruit would run. They had been paying and waiting for three years since that fateful day at Huntingdon. With fear and trepidation, the decision was made and with heavy hearts we watched Graham Thorner

canter The Fruit, splashing his way through the mud, down to the start to join the other eleven runners. We had a lift, however, for The Fruit had won his devoted lad, Ken, £25 for the best turned-out horse.

The Fruit jumped out of the gate and was well in front by the first fence. His bold jumping took him further and further ahead as he gained ground at each fence, jumping his rivals into the ground. He never looked like being beaten though he was a very tired horse as he crossed the line. We couldn't believe it. He had won like a good, sound horse—on bog-like going which he hated. There was no time to celebrate as I had a runner in the next and the

Graham Thorner with Forbidden Fruit race towards victory in the Beech Open Novices' Chase at Sandown

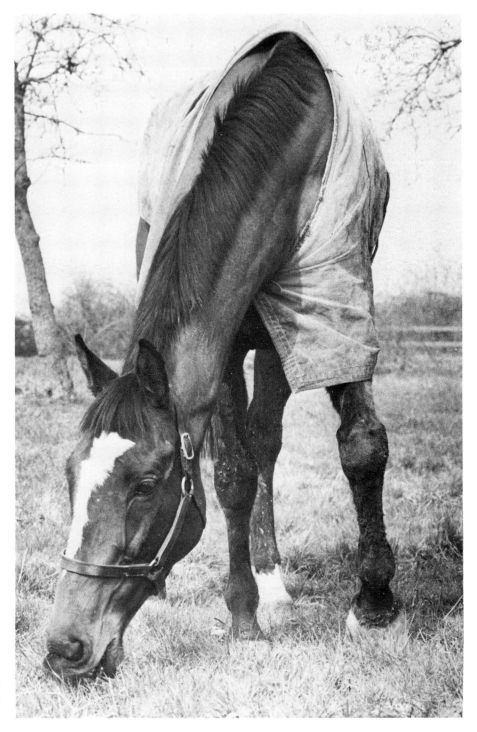

The Fruit relaxing at
the home of Patricia
Smyly

owners had to return to Doncaster. Anyhow, the only medicine needed would have been hot, sweet tea for shock. What a horse! He had done us proud. It was his courage and the devoted attention of many people that had carried him through, but above all the patience of his owners.

It was a wonderful moment for me and everybody else at Letcombe Bassett, especially as they had all seen the race on television, and in its way we all felt that it was a greater triumph than almost any other winner I had trained, including the Grand National victories of Well To Do and Ben Nevis. It was a triumph really just to have The Fruit fit and well again to run, let alone win.

The Fruit went on to finish second to the highly-rated Ten Dollars More at Sandown seventeen days later and ran six times in the following season, winning first time out at Newbury and finishing second on four other occasions. He then ran six times in the 1980–81 season, finishing second at Newbury and Chepstow, and third at Sandown before coming second in the Meynell Handicap Chase at Leicester on 2 March 1981.

His legs began to show a lot of wear and tear again and it was decided that he had done enough. He was sent back to his devoted friend, Patricia Smyly, to be hacked about, hunted and on 27 February 1982 he made his Hunter Chase debut in the Gay Sheppard Memorial Challenge Trophy at Stratford ridden by Dick Saunders who, five weeks later, won the Grand National on Grittar.

# JOSH GIFFORD

Whatever I may achieve in the future, nothing can surely compare with Aldaniti's fairy-tale win in the Grand National at Aintree on 4 April 1981.

Here was a horse that only eighteen months earlier I had thought would never be able to run again, being ridden by a jockey who two years earlier I had thought would never be able to ride again and owned by a man who seemed crazy even to consider putting him back in training . . .

And yet there was something almost unreal about Aldaniti for me from the very first day I set eyes on him at the Ascot Sales in May 1974. If it hadn't been for Mr Roger-Smith, my father-in-law, I wouldn't have even bought the horse; he nearly always came to the Sales with my wife Althea and myself when I first started training in 1970 because we felt three pairs of eyes were better than one. He was a good judge of horses but a bit old-fashioned and he kept me under control saying, 'You can't give that much for that horse, take a pull, take a pull, that's far too much . . .'

For some reason—don't ask me what—it was different with Aldaniti. He said, 'Come with me a minute, I've seen a horse you ought to buy.' I went and looked at the animal. Well, I didn't know what to think. He was a chestnut by Derek H and had no pedigree whatsoever but Mr Roger-Smith felt that if he didn't make a racehorse, he could be a fine event horse or show jumper. 'He's a lovely stamp of an individual with a good, honest head and, with any luck, you could not possibly lose money on him.'

He'd been bred by Tommy Barron at the Harrogate Stud and named after Tommy's four grandchildren, taking the first two letters of each, Alistair, David, Nicola and Timothy. But I thought he looked slow and made up my mind that I was only going to buy him if he was very cheap. Cheap in those days was about £1,200–£1,500 and I felt that would be plenty to give for him.

The bidding went on and on—I don't think he came on the market as it turned out until £1,500, so I went up to £2,000. It's one of those strange twists of fate, my father-in-law kept kicking me on, 'Go on, go on, have another one.' And just one more . . . so on I went, over a few more hurdles, suddenly he was mine—for £4,200! I do believe it was fate or call it what you like that we happened to get him as I had no real intentions of buying him in the first place.

Then reality sunk in. I began kicking myself, wondering what on earth I'd bought him for. We brought him back to Findon but my first reaction remained—he looked slow, he didn't really look a thoroughbred as a raw-boned four-year-old. He was big and strong but I kept thinking how slow he was going to be and wondering how I was going to sell him to an owner. You couldn't sell him on his pedigree—he had none! I showed him to a stack of people but no one was interested. So we decided to keep him ourselves and take a chance.

I had the Silver Doctor Novices Hurdle at Ascot on 10 January 1975 in mind for his first run. He was beginning to settle in his work on the gallops, although he was always in too much of a hurry and it was just a matter of teaching him to gallop faster—and, of course, to jump at speed. He'd been broken in and ridden round the farms at Tommy Barron's and jumping came naturally to him. He was always a little bit wooden in the sense that he had a hard mouth and used to pull quite hard. Very often, a horse that pulls hard doesn't go any faster when he comes off the bit which is the case with him, but luckily he is fast enough to be able to keep going; his heart's in the right place.

We were ready to run at Ascot and thought he just might surprise us but I didn't think we'd beat the Queen Mother's Sunyboy. Aldaniti jumped perfectly, made rapid headway at the fifth, led at the sixth and went away to beat Sunyboy into second place by four lengths. We were thrilled to bits. I knew now that we had a racehorse.

It had always been a bit of a gamble to run him. If he'd run badly, I don't know what we'd have done. Now it was different. I decided to try and get £5,000 for him. After all, I'd kept him for almost eight months and I didn't want to lose anything; though I didn't really want to make anything on him either.

That evening I rang Nick Embiricos, who'd had horses with me from the beginning and told him he ought to buy Aldaniti. He came over to see him next day and agreed to have him; I was just grateful for someone to pay the training bills. Little did we know, this was the start of a romantic journey.

Aldaniti ran four more times that season, finishing fourth in the Sun Alliance Novices Hurdle at the Cheltenham Festival to Davy Lad—with Sunyboy second and Express Mail third. We didn't start him off the following season until the Touchen End Handicap Hurdle at Windsor on 1

The morning before
the fairy-tale
National . . . Josh
Gifford, Bob
Champion and
Aldaniti

January 1976 where he was third before going to Sandown nine days later for the William Hill Handicap Hurdle. He finished sixth . . . and then the heartache began.

There was a little bit of warmth in his leg two or three days after the race. We kept our fingers crossed, hoping it was just a knock or a bang—but it wasn't; it was a strain. We didn't want to take a chance, he'd already shown us enough by then and Mrs Embiricos said, 'Don't let's kid ourselves the heat is not there when it is. We've had a warning, let's give him twelve months off.' They are marvellous owners, patient people with horses. So he went to the Embiricos's Barkfold Manor Stud nearby at Kirdford and was bar fired. The tendons are like a piece of elastic and, when you strain them, it's just a matter of tightening them up again and getting the blood running through the scar tissue. You usually fire them on both legs just to be safe and that's what they did with Aldaniti.

He came back to Findon in November 1976 as fat as a bull naturally—but looking fantastic. I'd got used to him by now. It takes you a while to get to know a horse; they're all different. We had a couple of months on the roads with Aldaniti and once we had him fit enough, we schooled him over fences. He was a bit erratic over one or two because he was so bold. He would not relax in those days; he was keen and enthusiastic but on the whole jumped well.

We chose the Sapling Novices' Chase at Ascot on 16 February 1977 for his first run over fences and I just wanted him to get through it safely and hoped his legs would stand the strain. I was delighted as it turned out—he finished second to Tree Tangle. I wasn't so happy at Newbury a couple of weeks later for Bob Champion literally fell off him! But Bob redeemed himself at Cheltenham where they were seventh in the Sun Alliance Chase before going on to win at Ascot and Uttoxeter in April and finish second at Fontwell.

We began the following season by winning the 2½-mile Leicestershire Silver Fox Handicap Chase at Leicester on 14 November and, as Bob dismounted, he said to me, 'We will win a National on him.' I didn't agree—I thought he was too erratic a jumper; he still made the odd mistake and was a bit free; too ignorant at that stage to jump round Aintree. But Bob never wavered in his judgement from that day in November 1977—and heaven knows, there was enough drama and heartache to come.

The next disappointment came in the Hennessy at Newbury on 26 November. Bob annoyed the horse's owners and myself by putting up 7 lbs overweight to start with and the race turned into a nightmare. Bob dropped him out as he was inclined to do in those days and he made an awful mistake at the second, he lost his hindlegs completely and literally was skidding along the ground. That put him right out of the race but Bob thought he was all right and they'd just go and jump a couple of fences to give him his confidence and then pull him up. He jumped them perfectly so Bob thought they'd go on for a couple more; he seemed fine. They kept on and were gradually in sight of the others. By the time they turned into the straight, he'd caught them and came to the last with a real chance. But then he ran out of gas halfway up the run-in and we had to settle for third place behind Bachelor's Hall and Fort Devon.

Aldaniti seemed perfectly all right after the race; he pulled up sound. But he was very lame back home at Findon—and still very lame the next morning. We couldn't find out where though. He seemed to be lame behind but we didn't know whether it was up in his back or what. We had different vets come and look at him but just couldn't get him sound. He was a little puffy around one joint and after about three or four weeks we thought we'd better have it X-rayed. It provided the answer—he'd chipped two of his bones on either side of the joint; the strain and pressure of trying to stop himself falling had undoubtedly caused it. It had taken us almost a month to diagnose the trouble—so back he went to Nick and Valda's for another six months in his box while the little chips floated back into position—which in itself was luck.

That's tough on a racehorse. A horse cannot be told to lie and rest so you just keep them on cold mash and hay so that they are not having any hard food to get them excited or worked up—but Aldaniti was a fantastic patient. He'd stand there in his box all day, day after day; never a moment's trouble.

He had just over a year off the track this time. By then he was difficult to place and we went straight for the King George on Boxing Day 1978 and finished sixth without ever looking like winning. But he'd showed us he was sound again and went on to have a terrific season, finishing third in the Gold Cup behind Alverton and Royal Mail, winning at Sandown and Haydock and finishing second to Fighting Fit in the Scottish Grand National at Ayr on 21 April.

And that was the moment when I began to think of him as a Grand National horse. He was unlucky not to win the Scottish National in that we didn't make enough use of him. I told Bob to drop him out because we weren't absolutely certain he'd stay the four miles and the ground was plenty fast enough for him. Bob had him settled beautifully and he was in a perfect position going down the back; in retrospect, he should have kicked on then for Fighting Fit came and did us for speed after we'd jumped the last in front. But we were still delighted and I began to think in terms of the 1980 National.

Bob by then had been pestering the owners every time he saw them. He'd go to them and say, 'How's that National horse of yours?' And Nick would ring me and say, 'I've seen Bob at the races today and he wants to know how Aldaniti is, he says he'll win a National.' Now, for the first time, I began to think Bob was right.

Then, in the summer of 1979, Bob was told he had cancer . . . we didn't know what to think; and, as the months went by, I was convinced he would never ride again. I told him his job was always there when he was ready to come back; my heart told me he'd never make it . . .

My owners were marvellous. I think loyalty is everything. You must be loyal to your staff and, after all, Bob, as stable jockey, is really part of the staff. Our job was to try and keep Bob's morale up and I knew that the thought of riding Aldaniti in the National was the one thing that was keeping him going through all the pain. So events at Sandown on 30 November 1979 were even more shattering than they might otherwise have been.

Richard Rowe rode Aldaniti—the only time Bob hasn't been on him, incidentally, apart from the Whitbread Trial Handicap Chase at Ascot in February 1982 and the following month's Greenall Whitley Breweries Handicap Chase when Bob was injured and Ron Barry took over—in what looked an ordinary enough race, the Ewell Handicap Chase over 3 miles 5 furlongs with only four runners. On reflection that was probably plenty far enough for his first run of the season but I thought they'd go nice and steady and that would suit him. He took it up at the fourth, quickened at the fourteenth and was absolutely cantering; it wasn't a question of whether he'd win but by how far . . .

Then, in two strides, he was pulled up lame on his near fore. I couldn't believe it. I ran down the course and met Richard just after the last fence; it was heartbreaking. Aldaniti was as lame as a cat, his tendon was so badly strained his fetlock joint was on the ground, it looked very bad. It seemed as if the kindest thing to do would be to put him down. But Aldaniti's owners are different. I knew they wouldn't even consider anything like that; they would want to take him home and give him every possible chance, even if he was going to be a cripple and be turned out in a field, they would look after him. Nonetheless, I was convinced he would never run again.

All I could think about was getting him back to Findon. He must have been in agony. It was a long, miserable drive home and, apart from anything else, I knew Bob would be shattered. Aldaniti looked a sorry sight that night: we put on a very tight bandage and kept it on until the swelling had settled down. When he was fit enough, on Thursday 13 December 1979, we loaded him up carefully and sent him back to Barkfold Manor . . . I never thought I'd see him at Findon again.

Althea and I were having dinner with Nick and Valda one evening in the summer of 1980 when Nick turned to me and said, 'You are going to have Aldaniti back.' I replied, 'Don't be so silly, Nick, he'll never stand training.' But Nick was insistent. 'I think he will,' he said. 'We are going to give him a chance. Bob's been ill and Bob wants to have another crack.' I was flabbergasted. 'Okay, if you really want to, I'd love to have him back but you are probably wasting your money.' Nick, ever the optimist, said, 'We probably are, but let's have a go. We'll go and win the National with him!' Althea and I drank to that . . .

They got up Aldaniti in the October and Valda had him for weeks on the road, walking and trotting, walking and trotting; she rode him quite a lot herself.

He came back to me on 22 December; not into his usual box but in one in the main yard next to Royal Judgement. I had one aim in mind—to get

Aldaniti to the National. I thought we'd give him perhaps one race before, though I felt I could get him fit enough without a race if necessary so long as his legs would stand it.

I decided that I would ride him in all his work. I didn't want to wrap him in cotton wool, I just felt that if anything went wrong then I couldn't blame any of my staff. He's got a wonderful temperament and I'd got to know him very well by now and I like to think I had the experience. If anything, he tries too hard; he wants to please too much.

Our horses are fed at six o'clock and first lot are ready to go out at 7.30—Aldaniti and I went with them. If the string were doing faster work, I went out the back or a long way in front and just took the pace very steadily, gradually moving on to the faster work and then only if the ground was absolutely perfect for him. If it was too firm or too wet, I just went trotting round the hills instead of cantering him. We're lucky with the ground at Findon: if it pours with rain for twelve hours, the horses cut through the grass on to the flints; but we know that if we don't get any more rain for twenty-four hours, it dries up and we've got perfect ground the following day. You don't have to work just for the sake of it. The younger horses have to be taught to gallop—you've got to be working them; but the older horses know how to gallop and jump and you can do just as much work with them trotting up and down the hills.

Aldaniti reminded me very much of Kilmore, who was a bit thick and would lean on you and pull and want to go faster than he could all the time. He'd jump three fences at home and all he'd want to do was go flat out instead of enjoying himself and having a jumping exercise; he'd want to race and tear about. I remember schooling him one day after racing at Hurst Park and I've never had such a hairy ride in all my life; yet Kilmore jumped round Liverpool three times. Aldaniti has just the same temperament.

So I never galloped Aldaniti with any other horse; I knew he'd want to go and race if he had anything else upsides. He always takes a good hold, especially when they're cantering in the string. And his legs? They seemed better than ever, it was incredible. I don't know whether it was just that he was much older or what, but they were harder certainly.

Everything went perfectly, I could hardly believe it. The more work we did, the better his legs seemed to be. He was beginning to go very well and lose his tummy and it then became a question of picking the right race for him before the National.

I still tried to keep a sense of proportion but Nick was already getting excited—and he wanted to have a bet on him even then, and he hadn't run. I told him candidly, 'Don't be silly, it's 66–1 him even getting there, let alone winning it.' Nick wouldn't have it; he's not a betting man but he likes a bit of fun—and he wanted his bit of fun. 'I don't believe it,' he said. 'You've got to be an optimist in this game.' He and Valda were in Jamaica when a bookmaker I'd approached about the bet rang, saying we could have what we liked at 66–1. I didn't know what to do. Althea was in the kitchen washing up the breakfast things. 'Halve the bet,' she said. So I did—and Nick was on at 66–1 . . . £250 each way. I knew Nick would split it up amongst his friends and play around with it but even so, I still thought he was crazy.

I had Aldaniti entered in two races in the second week of February—the Whitbread Trial Handicap at Ascot on Wednesday the 11th and the Harwell Handicap at Newbury two days later, Friday the 13th! We decided to go to Ascot—I felt we should take the first race that came along with decent ground. I didn't want to take the chance of waiting. You never know what might happen; you can be under a couple of feet of snow within twenty-four hours at that time of the year and we'd reached the stage where we wanted to have a run.

Bob came down and popped him over half a dozen fences; he generally came down to Findon to ride work if there was a two-day meeting at Sandown or Lingfield but with Aldaniti it was different; he'd have dropped everything and come straight down if I'd rung him one morning and said, 'Today's the day to school him.'

Looking back, it was a very hot contest to run him in; over 3 miles against seven, race-fit opponents and with 11 st 7 lbs to carry. I told Bob to drop him out and try and get him settled, not to bring him off the bridle and to bring him back in one piece; that was solely his mission. We didn't care where he finished, if he was placed second or third, well, that was a bonus but he must be brought back in one piece.

I suffered agonies before the race but, once they got going, I could hardly believe what I saw . . . it was so perfect. The horse was unbelievable; he did everything so well, jumped splendidly apart from a slight mistake at the last first time round, had a nice run into the straight and then took it up between the last two and absolutely cruised home by four lengths from Royal Charley with the Irish horse Kilkilwell third.

It was more than we had dared hope for in our wildest dreams and I knew then we needn't run him again before the National. If he was fit enough to go and beat those horses without a run, he'd be all right for Aintree—and, as far as I was concerned, for Cheltenham. I was keen to run him in the Gold Cup. I thought it was going to be a bad Gold Cup; my fancy at the time was for Tied Cottage and if you fancy an old horse like that, it's got to be a bad Gold Cup. I reckoned wherever Tied Cottage finished, we'd be in front; I didn't think Silver Buck would act on the soft or get the trip and I couldn't

see Little Owl winning; after all, novices don't win Gold Cups and Little Owl was only a novice.

Nick would have none of it. He'd been third in the Gold Cup and it didn't mean anything to him to be first or second in it. 'No, it's the National and nothing else,' he insisted. And he wouldn't even let me keep Aldaniti in at the four-day stage. As it turned out, Nick was right. It was a good Gold Cup and I don't think we'd have been in the first three and I was very wrong about Little Owl who is so clearly a very good horse, despite his problems during the 1981–82 season.

So it was the National—and nothing else. He came back sound from Ascot, the head lad took off his bandages the morning after and said, 'You feel those legs, I think they are better than before he went.' He'd had a very easy race and he's a very clean-winded horse, too, and we knew we needn't give him another race.

Then the weights came out and we had another surprise. We were delighted to get 10st 13lb for I feared we might get 11st 5 or 6lb. It was the ideal weight for Bob. Sometimes, the handicapper murders a horse but this time he was very fair—he'd given a good horse a good chance of winning a good race.

It was now just a matter of keeping him right, doing enough work but not too much and keeping him sound. So I did plenty of hill work, walking and trotting up hills and a lot of long, steady canters. I often sent the string off to do fast work and went off on another gallop with him, cantering him alone because I knew he would take less out of himself if he were on his own. I didn't want him to overdo himself. Then I popped him in the box a couple of times and took him over to Guy Harwood's all-weather gallop at Pulborough. Guy's very good like that, letting me use his gallop although I try not to abuse it. I thought Aldaniti would like a change; he'd got to know our gallops and naturally he knew where to expect to be galloped so the change did him good. It kept him alert and didn't disappoint him and I was able to get him to do just that little bit extra without him realising it. But I still didn't gallop him with anything else. He was always on his own.

As the National approached, the tension increased, and the build up only served to increase the pressure. The media had started to take a big interest in us—what with Bob having recovered from cancer and Aldaniti having been a virtual cripple himself. I found it difficult to sleep and Althea had to give me a couple of pills at night to help me relax.

Then, with only seventy-two hours to go we had a real scare. There was an outbreak of foot and mouth disease on the Isle of Wight and talk of zoning if there was another outbreak; we had the vets and the local policeman on the alert to let us know if there was any question of their not

*Opposite page*
Aldaniti strides up to the post to win the 1981 Grand National. 'That victory meant so much to so many people,' said Josh Gifford

letting horses out of the area. My vet rang on the Wednesday night to say he'd heard there was a possible case nearby at Sompting and advised me to get Aldaniti out of the way quickly. My first batch of runners had already left for the opening day of the Aintree meeting; Aldaniti was due to go up on Thursday.

I raced down the road to the Vale where the horses boxes are kept and got a box but couldn't find a driver, so I drove it up to our yard where our head lad Ron and secretary Judy together with Althea were tearing around with tools, hay and corn which got slung into the box.

Aldaniti was halfway through his evening feed but we hurriedly got him ready and he literally had one foot on the ramp when my vet tore up the drive to say it was only a scare and we were all clear. By this time, the various lads had been contacted and were arriving in the yard. One was heard to say, 'Okay, boys, it was only a rehearsal, we'll do it in ten minutes next time!' I didn't sleep too well that night. . . .

So to Liverpool—and heartbreak even then. Stonepark, another horse owned by Mr and Mrs Embiricos, was fatally injured in the Topham Trophy. It crossed my mind that they might pull Aldaniti out of the National—after all, Alverton, who was owned by Valda's relatives had been killed in the National in 1979. I wasn't going to mention it to them—and they never discussed it with me, but I know they talked about it themselves that night. But they love the game, they understand racing, and they know how to take the rough with the smooth.

Friday night was a happier occasion. Their children had joined them and about twenty of us went to a quiet restaurant in Southport—well, it was quiet until we took over! We had a riotous time. Monty Court, the *Sunday Mirror*'s racing correspondent, had us in stitches with one hilarious story after another.

We were all anxious to keep Bob calm. By then, I think there was enormous pressure on him, and we wanted to try and instil in him that it was just another race. It wasn't of course. . . . There were times when I told Bob 'You've got to win this one.' But this was different; he'd been through so much and this meant so much to him, I didn't want to add to the pressure. Nick and I tried to keep him up drinking when we got back to our hotel but he was first to bed. We were all up early and out on the course first thing Saturday morning. There's something special about Aintree on National morning. The owners are there . . . the trainers are there . . . the jockeys are there . . . the public are already getting there. We had Aldaniti out and gave him a canter—he looked superb. Then we walked every inch of the course and decided how we would run our race.

The inside had been cut up very badly in the Topham and there were great lumps out in places. We decided that Bob would line up on the outside; the fences are smaller on the outside anyway and, if all went well, the plan was to take it up at Becher's second time and kick on from there.

We returned to the Royal Clifton, had some toast, another three bottles of champagne, changed, paid the bill and made our way back to the racecourse. And everything went just perfectly. Usually I'm late or Althea's late and we're in a panic, but this time nothing went wrong. It was unusual and uncanny somehow . . .

Nick insisted on driving in our car because he'd dreamt he went with us—by then emotion had taken over, of course. There was nothing more we could do. We fancied our chances so much and everything had gone according to plan and yet we had this terrible feeling that something must go wrong.

We arrived at the course at 1 o'clock and Althea gave our son, Nicholas, strict instructions not to wander off and get lost. He did—and we never saw him after we went into the parade ring for the National until David Nicholson, who is his godfather, lifted him over the crowds and into the winner's enclosure . . .

I saw Nicky Henderson, the trainer of Zongalero, down at the start and we promised each other a dinner if either of us won but by that stage, you just want to get it over with. A friend of ours, Henry Pelham, had gone up onto the stand an hour before the race and saved us a place right at the far end nearest the start—and then they were off.

The rest, in many ways, is a blur. I saw Bob jump the first all right, then the second—and he made a mistake, just as Bob had hoped, for it pulled him up and taught him a lesson that the fences needed respect. After that, well . . .

My hands were shaking, I couldn't keep my glasses still and Nick was shouting at me, 'How's he doing, how's he doing?' 'He's fine,' I told him, 'jumping super, going great.' Truth is, I couldn't see him, the commentary hadn't picked him up either. Until the 11th, and then there was no mistaking him when he actually jumped past Zongalero and into the lead at the 12th. From then on, I never lost sight of him. Of course, we hadn't expected to be in front so soon but I'd told Bob if his jumping got him in front to keep on and not give it back to them.

Out in front and more than a circuit to go . . . my mind was racing. Yet the further they went, the better Bob and Aldaniti seemed to be going . . . he was jumping beautifully while the rest seemed to need more effort to get over those fearsome fences . . . I could see Aldaniti's head bobbing along, he was enjoying himself . . . two fences to go and Royal Mail made a mistake . . . one to go, up and over and now that long, murderous run-in . . . it seemed to

Home to Findon, the
day after Aintree

go on forever . . . I could see John Thorne and Spartan Missile putting in a
great run. Generally, I'll say to Althea, 'We've won this,' well before the
line; this time I didn't dare say a word. And then came the post . . . we'd
won, we'd done it . . . there was pandemonium. And tears. Floods of tears.
This meant so much to so many people.

It's difficult to remember the rest of that afternoon. It was two or three
hours before it really sunk it. We decided to be sensible afterwards; just a
couple of glasses of champagne and then back to Findon to see the race on
television that night. As it turned out, we realised we wouldn't make it and

stopped at a friend's house and saw it there. They were having a dinner party and were delighted for us to join them.

The next day was out of this world; the phone didn't stop ringing; everyone came up from the village and from Worthing, too, to see Aldaniti arrive home from Liverpool; there were drinks everywhere, the place was like a madhouse. I'll never forget it.

I'll always treasure all the letters I received from all kinds of people from all walks of life . . . one from Major Dick Hern, who has trained goodness knows how many Classic and big race winners, that meant a lot to me.

I don't want to take all the credit: first, there was my father-in-law's judgement and then there was Nick and Valda's patience. They gave Aldaniti the time to give me what is truly my Greatest Triumph.

# GUY HARWOOD

To-Agori-Mou will always be special to me and his victory in the Two Thousand Guineas at Newmarket on 2 May 1981 was especially sweet because it was very much a team effort. It involved so many people in a big way—my brother-in-law and assistant, Geoff Lawson, jockey Greville Starkey, the head lad Tom Townsend and Steve Freeguard, the lad who looked after the horse, as well as my blacksmith Ron Warner and vet Brian Eagles. Everybody was so much involved, it was such a great triumph for everyone at Coombelands.

No one outside our stables in Pulborough, Sussex, knew what we'd been through to get the horse to Newmarket—let alone have him fit enough to win a Classic. That's why I've chosen To-Agori-Mou and the Guineas though other horses stick in my mind like Jan Ekels, who won the Trafalgar House Handicap at Ascot in September 1972 and the Queen Elizabeth II Stakes there the following year; like Ela-Mana-Mou, who I trained to win at Royal Ascot in 1979; like Young Generation, who really should have won the Two Thousand Guineas in 1979 but coughed six weeks before the race and ended up third before going on to win the Lockinge; like Recitation who won the French Guineas in 1981 and like a horse called Michel Andrew, who I trained to win over hurdles, over fences and on the Flat all within a year.

Michel Andrew started the sequence by winning the 2-mile Sticklepath Selling Handicap Hurdle at Newton Abbot on 27 August 1966, took the 2-mile Watton Novices Chase at Fakenham on 10 September—both times being ridden by Josh Gifford—and then won the Dauntsey Selling Handicap over a mile at Bath on 9 June 1967. That was quite something and Michel Andrew was only a small horse!

Max and Andry Muinos have owned both Ela-Mana-Mou and To-Agori-Mou; Ela-Mana-Mou was a top-class mile and a half colt whereas To-Agori-Mou had the speed and acceleration to win the Two Thousand

Guineas. We bought To-Agori-Mou as a yearling at the Newmarket September Sales in 1979 specifically for Mrs Muinos, who had by then sold Ela-Mana-Mou. It was one of those cases where James Delahooke, who helps me buy the horses and is an excellent judge of an athlete which is the important thing, and I both had no doubts that he was the yearling we should buy. He'd been consigned by Rathduff Stud from whom we'd bought Young Generation two years before so we had good reason to think that Josephine Edwards was breeding good horses. I think that the hotel they come from is very important; he was an exceptional individual, the outstanding colt at the Sales. He was by Tudor Music and made 20,000 guineas, the valuation we had set on the horse.

The early days of a potential racehorse are vital. We bring the yearlings into the yard when the Flat season is over and To-Agori-Mou came into training three weeks after he was broken; the yearlings are ridden six days a week and it's all education from there on.

The first six months that a yearling/two-year-old is in training is a period primarily for development of his heart and lungs, general maturity of his body, bone development and producing the horse in a fit condition for his first appearance on the racecourse. During this time he is mouthed, broken, broken to the saddle and to the human being on his back, taught to lead with his inside leg depending on the direction in which he goes, developing the balance to learn how to canter and gallop upsides with his companions, how to cope with starting stalls and everything which is going to be expected of him on the racecourse.

The first six months of his life therefore, in a racing stable is very important and can fashion his future attitude to racing. During this period, you are feeding the horse for development and growth as well as energy to enable him to keep up with his day-to-day training; therefore, feeding of a young horse is vitally important, much more important than for a mature, developed horse. He must have the best food available to enable him to mature as quickly as possible.

To-Agori-Mou was one of the few horses that always looked like a top-class horse though he looked as though he was going to need time. I started to train him reasonably hard in May and early June 1980 but had to stop for a month because he was becoming a little excited by it all. I felt that if I wasn't careful he might, what we call, boil over and get too excited by racing and worry about it, though he eventually developed a much better temperament than I expected and once he seemed to get the message of what it was all about, took to racing extremely well.

He had his first race in the Fulbourn Stakes over 6 furlongs at Newmarket on 10 July, disputing the lead from the start with the Queen's Church

Guy Harwood . . .
'To-Agori-Mou will
always be special to
me.'

Parade, who was trained by Dick Hern, and going down by three-quarters of a length with Ardar third. After that, To-Agori-Mou progressed much more quickly than I had anticipated. He had become a little excited in the stalls at Newmarket and I gave him two easy races to develop his confidence. He won the 7-furlong Foxhall Stakes at Goodwood on 30 July by two lengths from Clear Verdict and was 3–1 on for Lingfield's 7-furlong Crawley Stakes, which was a very easy contest, on 8 August where he coasted in again by two lengths from Campton.

I was anxious not to give him a hard race too soon and though the Champagne Stakes would have been ideal, I didn't want to be tempted into running him too high too soon. We went instead for the 7-furlong Intercraft Solario Stakes at Sandown on 29 August and once more he won by two lengths from Bold Raider. Then we rested him before the William Hill Dewhurst Stakes at Newmarket on 17 October, his last race as a two-year-old.

To-Agori-Mou did a marvellous gallop at Lingfield before the Dewhurst with Rankin and a horse called Big Pal, who led the way; Rankin had been third in the 1980 Derby to Henbit and was in fact fourth in the Champion Stakes behind Cairn Rouge, Master Willie and Nadjar the day after the

Dewhurst. There was no doubt that To-Agori-Mou was an exceptional horse in the Lingfield gallop and I couldn't see him being beaten at Newmarket. As it was, we had a tremendous battle with Vincent O'Brien's Storm Bird, who beat us by half a length. Storm Bird was then rated top of the Free Handicap with 9st 7 lbs while To-Agori-Mou was given 9st 6 lbs and my other two good colts, Recitation and Kalaglow 9st 1 lb and 8st 10 lbs respectively.

I had made up my mind by then that To-Agori-Mou would be my Guineas horse for 1981; I always felt he would be a top-class miler; he could handle fast, good or soft ground. Without doubt, he had absolute brilliance and a very good temperament and, barring an accident, looked the one horse who could beat Storm Bird. As it turned out, of course, Storm Bird never ran as a three-year-old until the middle of September after a series of mishaps. Recitation was the other obvious contender; he loved soft ground and liked Longchamp so it was sensible to aim him at the French Two Thousand Guineas. I never felt at any time that Recitation was a better horse than To-Agori-Mou; I won't say he wasn't as good, but he was never a better horse.

To-Agori-Mou came back into full training in the middle of November and then it was simply a process of conditioning right through until the middle of February when we start half speed, serious work. Unfortunately, he tore a muscle in his quarters and we had to give him a week off at the end of February which was almost disastrous because he needed a lot of work. All the weight we'd taken off him went back on and we had to start all over again. Fortunately, he did not have a recurrence of that muscle trouble but he was quite stiff in the mornings when he was first pulled out; it was a worry but we had to live with it. Psychologically, you've then got to persuade a horse to use himself, but after that he was for some time fairly stiff for the first five minutes.

Everything then went relatively smoothly except that he was plenty heavy enough and because of the hold-up I decided to delay his first race until the Craven at Newmarket on Tuesday 14 April, just eighteen days before the Guineas. It was perfectly placed, we were guaranteed good ground and it gave me just those extra few days with the horse. Greville Starkey came and rode him in his work with Recitation and Kalaglow; it's an enormous help to have three first-class horses to carry each other through their work. Recitation trotted up in the Two Thousand Guineas Trial at Salisbury on 4 April and that gave us great encouragement for To-Agori-Mou who always seemed to have that little spark of brilliance on top of the others although he was a very gross horse and always blew much harder than them.

But that first week of April stopped us in our tracks because To-Agori-

Mou tore off a shoe and a large portion of his near fore with it; we had to stop again, this time for five days during which he couldn't be ridden. This was just about the worst thing that could happen at that stage and we had enormous difficulty getting the shoe back on his foot; we had to build it up with plastic—and the Craven was getting closer and closer. When a horse has had five days off, you can't go straight back on the gallops immediately because they only get tied up, similar to a human cramp, so you've got to start cantering and we were only able to get two bits of work into him before the Craven.

We had to run him if we were going to make the Guineas and we thought he had enough brilliance to get away with it, but every time we shod him, there was soreness in his foot and he was lame for twelve hours. So we had a very difficult problem, but I decided to go ahead. We had to shoe him the day before the Craven and certainly he was sore until he got loosened up and warmed up. As it turned out, I suppose he ran a super race in going down by only three-quarters of a length to Kind of Hush. Greville didn't murder the horse but he was riding an animal who was athletically exhausted. Fortunately, we'd been able to keep the problem to ourselves though one obviously said afterwards that we'd had a hold-up.

It is interesting here perhaps to talk about the horse's weight for I take great care with my horses and their weight. To-Agori-Mou was 1,090 pounds when he ran in the Dewhurst—we weigh them with a set of tack—and by the following January he was around 1,170; he'd come down to 1,130 by the middle of March and was around 1,120 when he ran in the Craven. I wanted him back to 1,090 for the Guineas and, in fact, he was spot on. I was confident I had him right as a two-year-old and I usually find that to get a horse fit at the beginning of his three-year-old career, he needs to be the same weight as he was at the end of his two-year-old career. It's no good, of course, getting a horse's weight right at the expense of the horse, you must do it gradually; if you start rushing it, you do more harm than good so I wasn't perturbed therefore that To-Agori-Mou was overweight for the Craven. I expected that in view of the hold-up in his training.

Everything went extremely well then. He did not miss a day's exercise, we have three work mornings a week at Coombelands though To-Agori-Mou did more than that before the Guineas, of course. He was led out on 15 April, ridden out on the 16th for one canter, and again on the 17th. He did two canters on the 18th and a swinging canter, about twenty miles an hour, on the 19th.

The horse had another slightly stronger piece of work than a swinging canter on 20 April and worked a sharp four furlongs; he did the same again on the 21st. The purpose was to prepare him for a gallop the following day

where we worked him with Recitation, who was due to run at Longchamp in the Poule d'Essai des Poulains, The French Two Thousand Guineas. Rankin, ridden by my brother-in-law Geoff Lawson, led the work with Greville on To-Agori-Mou and Mark Perrett on Recitation. Greville was weighted so that he was giving around five pounds to the older horse, Rankin, and he was around two pounds heavier than Recitation. Rankin led them a good gallop all the way up the Valley Gallop which is a six-and-a-half furlong all-weather strip; To-Agori-Mou worked the best of the party while Rankin and Recitation at the weights worked out about the

To-Agori-Mou (right) storms to victory in the 1981 Two Thousand Guineas

same. It was an incredibly good gallop and since Recitation then went on to slaughter the French horses, it gave us great encouragement for To-Agori-Mou.

The horse did his first canter and another swinging canter on the 23rd, and on the 24th he worked at a sharp racing pace over five furlongs; on the 25th he galloped six furlongs on the grass, unfortunately getting a little unbalanced and this was not a particularly pleasing piece of work. On the 26th, he did his first canter and a nice half-speed piece of work. On the 28th, with Greville on board, To-Agori-Mou galloped five furlongs in a really sharp piece of work, bowling along at racing pace. This was a very pleasing piece of work and his last serious gallop; after this, on the 29th and 30th, he did sharp work over four furlongs on both days. Then he travelled to Newmarket on Friday, 1 May.

What a day that turned out to be! I was horrified when I heard the draw . . . number one in a field of nineteen. I could have cried. If there is any sort of wind in the other direction at Newmarket, then a horse that is exposed on the outside will cop it the whole way. On top of this, To-Agori-Mou was better just covered in the early stages of a race; I'm not saying he wanted to be dropped out, but at least just have a lead. The draw was the really big worry I had and we were all in a tremendously nervous state by then because we'd been under a lot of pressure, not unpleasant pressure but pressure from the media particularly, who couldn't see why we were so confident after being beaten in the Craven.

I was naturally very keen to win the Guineas and the problems with the horse had added to that pressure. Greville was the one person who remained calm, outwardly anyway, throughout the whole thing and managed to keep a sense of sanity. He was so confident that he was going to win; he knew exactly what he wanted to do and how he wanted to ride the horse. We trainers rely so much on our jockeys and work riders to give us the right information when they ride the horse; we are very largely in their hands and there is none better than Greville.

It didn't help my nerves much, however, when I saw To-Agori-Mou come out of his box at Newmarket after travelling from Pulborough. We were still building up his foot with plastic, of course, and we had the vet and blacksmith there in case there were problems; we were still worried about that aspect of things. He pulled out extremely crotchety and took four lame steps because he'd been standing so long. It was an agonising moment, but a fleeting one fortunately, for he was perfectly all right as soon as he stepped on grass.

I slept soundly on Friday night and To-Agori-Mou was fine when I went up to the stables before seven the next morning; I saw him out and he was in

*Opposite page*
Owner Max Muinos greets Greville Starkey and To-Agori-Mou after their triumph

good form. There's nothing more to be done at that stage though I always like to be down at the parade before a big race because this is an area where things can go wrong. If you were up in the stands and something went wrong in the parade, you'd never get back down. I like to see the horse canter off and Greville says he sometimes thinks I'm going to canter down with him! But once they turned and went down towards the start, I made my way to the lad's head-on stand for the climax to all the days, weeks and months of work and worry.

You don't get the best view of a race head-on, but I was happy enough once they jumped off. The plan was for Greville to track across the whole time to have some horses to race with and get some cover; he did it perfectly and the horse showed tremendous courage as they ran through the Dip and To-Agori-Mou held off Mattaboy by a neck with Bel Bolide one length and a half away third; although there was a photograph, I was confident we'd won . . . and Greville had no doubt at all!

That was a special moment but an exceptional day for me was topped off as I was saddling Taher for the Culford Stakes two races later; there was a knock at the stable door and it was Lord Porchester, who took me to be introduced to The Queen. I'd never met Her Majesty before and it was a great privilege and honour.

# CRIQUETTE HEAD

I could have danced all night after Three Troikas, owned by my mother Ghislaine and ridden by my brother Freddie, had won the Prix de l'Arc de Triomphe by three lengths from Le Marmot at Longchamp on Sunday, 7 October 1979 with the Epsom Derby winner Troy a further length back in third.

Who could blame me for rushing on to the track at the end of the race with tears running down my cheeks and arms raised aloft . . . I'd won the Arc in only my second season as a trainer. Wonderful!

My lovely Three Troikas, at that time beaten only once in seven starts, was the toast of France. I adored her. I'd adored her from the first time I set eyes on her as a foal. She had that undefinable special quality from the start and I had been determined to be involved in the filly's career.

Three Troikas began life at the Haras du Bois Roussel but shortly afterwards had the chance to be sent to the Haras de Roiville where breeder and ex-Panzer officer Arthur Pfaff, kept his broodmares and their produce. This delightful stud is owned and managed by one of France's great characters, the Danish-born Jorgen Permin. Three Troikas arrived at the Roiville in September 1976 and remained there until 15 July 1977 when she was sent to the Comte Roland de Chambure's Haras d'Etreham to be prepared for the sales. In correspondence as early as December 1976, Permin was already stating that he had a potential 'crack' at his stud. He, too, had been completely struck with the filly from the start. 'It was never a surprise to me that Three Troikas turned out to be a champion. She was born a fine specimen, always ate bloody well and never stopped growing,' says Permin. Three Troikas was part of a record-breaking consignment submitted by the Haras d'Etreham to the 1977 Houghton Sales at Newmarket and the Stowe-educated Chambure is a close friend and business associate of my family. Produce presented by the Etreham, which is situated near Bayeux in Normandy, always fetch top prices and 1977 was no exception. I laid out 41,000 guineas to obtain Three Troikas. In fact, I was lucky. There was only a reserve on her of 40,000 guineas and I think many people were put off by her excessive tail swishing. I was determined to obtain Three Troikas and if my mother had not been willing to fork out the purchase price, then I'd have bought the filly for one of Maurice Zilber's patrons.

Three Troikas is by the Northern Dancer stallion Lyphard, who is remembered in England for his steering problems in the Epsom Derby, out of the moderate Dual mare Three Roses: she was sold out of Michael Connolly's yard at Tattersalls in 1970 having won a couple of small races at Navan and Phoenix Park as a two-year-old.

When I bought Three Troikas, I already knew I would be training her because Christian Datessen, after nearly thirty years with our family at the Villa Vimy stables, had decided to retire and my father, Alec, had agreed that I should replace him. Just as soon as she was broken, I began to see great quality in Three Troikas but we did not hurry her and she did not make her racecourse debut until the autumn of 1978. I discovered early on that Three Troikas was a sugar addict but a model pupil and exceptionally fond of her Tunisian-born lad, Amar Boussaffa. It was he who led Three Troikas round the paddock at Saint-Cloud on 20 November 1978 before she contested the Prix Messaline which was taken in greenish style from Zhetaire, who was to remain a maiden all her life.

By the time of the Prix Vanteaux the following April, the reputation of Three Troikas on the home gallops was pretty well known so it was no surprise to see her win by three lengths from Dunette, who was later to hand out the first defeat in the career of Three Troikas. Following this effortless victory, many people were comparing the filly with the legendary Allez France and how right they turned out to be. Although the Prix Vanteaux is run over a distance just short of 10 furlongs, I thought Three Troikas possessed enough speed and class to beat the best over the mile in the Poule d'Essai des Pouliches, the French One Thousand Guineas, on 29 April. Once again, Freddie brought Three Troikas with a challenge halfway up the straight and the pair went on to take the Classic by two and a half lengths from Nonoalca, the winner of the Group III Prix de la Grotte, and Waterway.

We began to build up to the Prix de Diane de Revlon in mid-June and turned out Three Troikas for the 10-furlong Prix Saint-Alary at Longchamp on 20 May where she was again to meet many old rivals so, barring accidents defeat was out of the question. Three Troikas, dominating her opponents from the entrance to the straight, strolled home by two lengths from Pitasia with Salpinx a further half-length behind and the rest nowhere.

It seemed inconceivable that Three Troikas could be beaten in the Prix de Diane on 10 June—but she was, by Dunette who hadn't had a look in behind Three Troikas in the Prix Saint-Alary and had been twelve lengths back in fifth. It became obvious before the straight that Three Troikas was not herself. Coupled with her pacemaker Sealy at 10–1 on, Three Troikas laboured her way past Nonoalca and Producer with two furlongs left, but could not hold the late flourish of Dunette who, with Georges Doleuze in the saddle, got up on the line to win by the minimum distance of a nose.

It was a heart-breaking moment. I felt awful. The crowd, not knowing the circumstances, booed as we led the filly in. They were unaware that my father and I knew that Three Troikas was not 100 per cent a fortnight before the race—Three Troikas jarred herself sometime after the Saint-Alary. Her feet were never her strong point but only Papa and I knew about the problem. Freddie never had any idea. Three Troikas was wearing boots in her box ten days before the Diane. It was a shame they blamed Freddie for the defeat. Maybe we shouldn't have run her. On dismounting, Freddie remarked that it was only 'sheer guts' that enabled Three Troikas to run so well; he had considered her beaten soon after the start.

Happily, Three Troikas was only very sore after the race but not

There's no catching Three Troikas as she races home in the 1979 Arc otherwise injured in any way but we were forced to give her an unscheduled holiday from racing until the Prix Vermeille in mid-September. I began to give Three Troikas some light work in mid-July and the plan was to build her up to a peak for the Prix de l'Arc de Triomphe. While Papa was in Normandy enjoying the delights of Deauville, I stayed at Chantilly to prepare Three Troikas for the Prix Vermeille which we considered an outing but not a target. The Group I event, run over the full Arc course, had attracted all Three Troikas' old rivals plus the Epsom Oaks heroine, Scintillate. At the end of the gruelling 1½ miles, Freddie and Three Troikas

Criquette Head greets brother Freddie and Three Troikas. 'I could have danced all night,' said Criquette

A lovely couple . . .
Criquette Head and
Three Troikas

were the short-head winners from the fast-finishing Salpinx and Pitasia. I was delighted. Three Troikas was terribly short of work and only fifty per cent fit. Even more important, she didn't hurt her feet.

Our family had three possible runners in the Arc and in the final gallop Freddie was on board Jacques Wertheimer's Gay Mecene, who earlier in the season had given a hiding to Ela-Mana-Mou in the Grand Prix de Saint-Cloud. The ever faithful Reginald Perkins, who has been with my family almost twenty-five years, was entrusted to Three Troikas and after the work I was convinced that, barring mishaps, Three Troikas was sure to win Europe's richest race. As the ground became soft, it was decided to send Gay Mecene for the Preis Von Europa, leaving the family represented by Three Troikas, ridden by Freddie of course, and the more than useful Fabulous Dancer.

Freddie, I realise, is a much abused jockey in England but he's been dreadfully unlucky and no one could have ridden Three Troikas better; he rode her to perfection. She was badly drawn in the field of twenty-two but Freddie made progress along the rails and had her close up from halfway; she cruised past the leaders below the distance and raced home unchallenged. Wonderful!

The rest of that day is something of a haze though I have fond memories of meeting the then French President Valéry Giscard d'Estaing who presented myself, my mother and Freddie with various *objets d'art*.

We had hoped that Three Troikas might return and win the Arc the following year but, after a series of mishaps, it came a little too soon for her but she ran a cracking race and finished fourth behind Detroit, Argument and Ela-Mana-Mou. She had anything but a trouble-free run and was always forced to race on the outside. We sold her in a multi-million deal in the summer of 1981 and she is now in Kentucky. I visited her when she was being prepared for the attentions of Exclusive Native; the sound of my voice and the mention of sugar had her in full gallop hurrying to say 'hello!'

Now I have one burning ambition: to win the Epsom Derby with a product of Three Troikas owned by my mother and ridden by Freddie who showed the English Press that he is not only brilliant round Longchamp when winning the Two Thousand Guineas at Newmarket on Zino on May Day, 1982.

# BARRY HILLS

Thirteen races as a two-year-old is not necessarily the ideal preparation for a horse with serious Classic potential—but that's what I did with Tap On Wood, who gave my American stable jockey Steve Cauthen an English Classic victory at only his second attempt in the Two Thousand Guineas at Newmarket on Saturday, 5 May 1979.

It was one of the most satisfying victories since I started training at South Bank, Lambourn, in 1969. Pat Hogan has always helped me select the yearlings and he was with me at Dublin Sales in 1977 when a grand-looking chestnut by Sallust out of Cat O'Mountaine by Ragusa took our eye, purely on his conformation. He had been bred by the Irish National Stud and we were delighted to buy him for £12,000 for Tony Shead. He was subsequently named Tap On Wood.

The more we saw of him, the more we liked him; he was a good walker, a nice easy-moving horse with a lot of quality about him. The only sad thing was that we left behind the horse in the next box. This turned out to be Kilijaro who, by coincidence, became the property of one of my owners, Nicholas Robinson. He was lucky enough to acquire her from Dermot Weld. She scored many successes in Europe before going on to even better things in America.

Tap On Wood was broken along with my other two-year-olds. They all gradually progressed towards their initiation into actual training. It became obvious when the string started to do a little work faster than a canter that Tap On Wood worried about the whole job and broke out in terrible sweats. He was a rather funky individual.

As a trainer, you spend a great deal of time with the horses which gives you the opportunity to study them closely as individuals. Every horse is different—some feed well, some don't; some are suited better by one rider than another. It is more or less intuitive what sort of programme you make out for any particular two-year-old. It's rather like a child in a classroom;

Barry Hills . . . 'The more we saw of Tap On Wood, the more we liked him.'

the teacher realises that he has ability but he is not actually producing it until the teacher finds the right way of delivering the message.

I have always believed in travelling my horses and reckon that teaches them a great deal. I decided that Tap On Wood should have his first race quite early in the season and he went to Newbury for the 5-furlong Beckhampton Stakes on 14 April 1978 and finished second, four lengths behind Kassak. Ten days later, he ran in the Hodcott Maiden Stakes at Bath, finishing fourth, beaten five and a half lengths by Bolide. This certainly didn't make him a very good horse at that time and it took him quite a few races to get going. He needed toughening up, but I knew that if I could stop him sweating, he would start to get stronger and carry more condition.

Fortunately, he was a horse that went on any kind of ground, but needed a tough pace throughout the race. He would never be likely to win a slowly-run race and I thought the best policy was to send him up the Great North Road every week to harden him up and that's the main reason why he ran so many times as a two-year-old.

It is interesting that he had a full brother called Americos which was a two-year-old in 1981. Vincent O'Brien had trouble with the horse because he was very nervy and sweaty and showed all the symptoms that Tap On

Wood had in his early two-year-old career. I rang Vincent's son-in-law, John Magnier, and suggested that he told Vincent to get on with the horse and run him every Saturday. He did just that and Americos gained two victories from three runs in just over three weeks.

Tap On Wood won seven of his thirteen races as a two-year-old, including two at Pontefract, one at Doncaster, one at Newbury and one at The Curragh. The 7-furlong National Stakes at The Curragh on Saturday, 2 September was far and away the highest class race in which he had run. There were thirty-four English entries that year, of which twenty-eight were trained by me. Breeders hadn't really taken full account of the race at that time although it was Group 2. I had done a bit of homework with my owners and, with the help of my secretarial staff, arranged for those entries to be made at the fairly nominal sum of £25. The value to the winner was £20,000.

Tap On Wood beat Dickens Hill a head in the National Stakes with Sandy Creek a length further away in third place. Both the second and third were known to be pretty good horses and it was clear that my fellow had improved enormously. I remember telling Tony Shead in the early winter that I thought Tap On Wood was sure to be placed in the next year's Guineas and might well win. Apart from the good form of the National Breeders' Stakes, I had a strong recollection of a horse of mine called Royal Manacle which had run fourth in the 1975 Guineas behind Bolkonski, beaten four lengths. I was convinced that Tap On Wood was a better horse and, granted a good run, could not see him out of the first three.

Ernie Johnson had ridden Tap On Wood in virtually all his races as a two-year-old and was indeed rather unfortunate not to ride him during his brief three-year-old career, but Steve Cauthen had come over from America to join our stable in March 1979. Tap On Wood wintered well and our eyes were firmly focused on the Guineas. His first race as a three-year-old was in deplorable ground in Salisbury's Two Thousand Guineas Trial Stakes on Saturday, 7 April and he finished fourth to Ryan Price's Lake City. He had in fact run quite a good race and from then on improved all the time.

We talked it over and decided that we would back the horse at 66–1 and we had quite a nice little touch—at that price you didn't need much on him, but I think I won something like £5,000 and Tony probably a bit more.

Tap On Wood went to Thirsk for the Timeform Race Card Stakes on 21 April—his first race over 1 mile. Although quite a small race, it had in fact attracted a useful field and Tap On Wood beat Abbeydale half a length with the other five runners nowhere.

His final preparation for the Guineas went very smoothly. He travelled to Newmarket the day before and was led out for three-quarters of an hour on

Tap On Wood (centre) holds off Kris (right) and Young Generation to win the 1979 Two Thousand Guineas

the morning of the race. I never work horses on racecourses on the day of racing except at Chester, where I am a great believer in giving them a sight of those tight bends. If they see them for the first time in the race, they are inclined to treat them over-cautiously. Steve had been on him in only the one previous race but had ridden him out several times at home, but Tap On Wood, being so lazy, had not shown him anything. The horse was now very calm and showed no sign of excitement in the preliminaries.

There were twenty runners and they went a real strong gallop. In the early stages Kris, the 15–8 favourite, and Tap On Wood, who started at 20–1,

Steve Cauthen and
Tap On Wood
entering the winner's
enclosure

were last and last but one, but they quickened up from about three and a
half furlongs out and the race was between the two until Young Generation
came on the scene; in fact, there was one desperate moment when I thought
Young Generation might beat them both, but our horse stuck to his job very
gamely and Steve gave him a great ride. Tap On Wood held off Kris by half a
length with Young Generation a short head away. With hindsight, the 1979
Guineas was almost certainly a very high-class event.

Tap On Wood was rather unlucky after that. We decided to let him take
his chance in the Derby on 6 June, even though we recognised that the

distance might be beyond his best; he had taken so little out of himself and was so relaxed we felt he might just get the trip. Steve chose him in preference to Two Of Diamonds and Cracaval and Bill Shoemaker came over from America to ride the latter; neither ran very well. Tap On Wood was possibly not at his best at the time of the Derby as all my horses went wrong with very poor blood counts. After the Derby, he was off the course until September when he went to Doncaster and won the Kiveton Park Steel Stakes from R. B. Chesne.

By then, the horse had become increasingly lazy at home. Snowy Outon, my head lad, liked to ride him out but if my wife Penny was at home, she nearly always did. I recall one morning working the horse over four and a half furlongs on Neardown with a bad maiden three-year-old—and the maiden beat him five lengths. I said to Penny, 'Look, if you can't make the horse go, I'll have to put somebody else on it—that's your last chance! You'll have to do better than that if, after winning the Guineas, you get beaten five lengths by a bad maiden!' She persevered and made the horse do a bit of work, but he would actually race with a donkey and I think that's probably one of the reasons he did so well—he was well able to conserve his energy and was a magnificent athlete.

Sadly, after the Doncaster race, Tap On Wood had a second dose of the virus which prevented him from running again.

It was a particular disappointment to all of us that he never had the chance to take on Kris again. It would have been a very good match in the Queen Elizabeth. I feel sure that his best distance was around a mile and he had won the Guineas on merit. Since he left my yard at the end of that season, I did not see him again for two years by which time he had developed into a magnificent stallion and grown about 1½ inches. I like to think that I found the solution to Tap On Wood's problems early in his two-year-old career and will always regard him as a very high-class miler.

# ARTHUR MOORE

Irian, once condemned to die because he was useless, was transformed in fifteen months at my stables at The Curragh into a brilliant, fluent-jumping winner of one of Ireland's most competitive races, the Sweeps Handicap Hurdle, at Leopardstown on Thursday, 27th December 1979; the very same horse who at first just wanted to stay in a field and wouldn't even leave the gate, let alone jump a twig.

It was marvellous, too, that my mother Joan and father Dan, who had enjoyed such triumphs with horses like L'Escargot, winner of the Cheltenham Gold Cup in 1970 and 1971 and then the Grand National in 1975, were able to share this success.

The story starts in 1976 when I had just begun training on a small scale and was also buying horses to send to England, mainly to Tim Forster and Andrew Wates. I had an advertisement in the *Irish Field* for some unbroken three-year-olds and among the replies was one from Raymond Keogh, a friend of my parents, who rang to say he had a three-year-old by Electrify. I told him I wouldn't be interested in an Electrify horse because he was close in breed to Nearco and I didn't think he was very good stuff for jumping and certainly not worth buying unbroken to go to England.

I thought nothing more about it but, two weeks later, Raymond rang and asked if I would train the horse; it was one thing buying it, quite another training it. I agreed immediately, and a year and a half later on 14 July 1978, Legal Switch won his fourth race for us at Down Royal, a 2-mile flat handicap.

Raymond invited my wife Mary and I for a meal at his home in Clonee just outside Dublin on the way home and took me down to the fields to see a little French horse which he'd come across a month earlier. Raymond's daughter had been working at Myrtle Allen's hotel in Cork and Yas Allen, the daughter of the hotel's proprietor, had been employed at Mick Bartholomew's stable in Chantilly looking after this particular horse who had won a couple of races as a three-year-old. His temperament had let him down and he'd burst blood vessels as well. They were going to put him down and Yas Allen had paid the price of whatever he'd make as meat money, about £300, and flew him back to Dublin. She had asked Mr Keogh if he could stay the night in his fields at Clonee near the airport before driving him back to Cork. The horse was Irian.

Raymond had rather taken to Irian and bought him for about £1,000, the girl having paid £500 to fly him over with the Sweeps Derby runners from France. At the time, Raymond had a head man who used to be with Ryan Price and he and his wife, very able horse people, had gelded Irian and let him out to grass; apparently, he hardly knew how to eat it, it was so long since he'd seen any. They gave him six weeks out and were planning to train him for Raymond as they had a licence to train privately.

I thought at the time he was a sweet little horse, not very big, but that was that as far as I was concerned. Two months later, Raymond came up to me at The Curragh and asked if I would take Irian because he was proving difficult to handle, he wouldn't even leave the yard.

He was a bit of a lad when he arrived and he wasn't keen to even leave the gateway when he went into a field to canter. It was obvious that he had been soured, possibly by too much work in France, and he was frightened that we were going to do the same with him. My father had quite a few horses sent to him with similar problems, including Antique which Jack Dawbin sent him from Chantilly in the mid-fifties and went on to win a Galway hurdle, and Bahrain which Snowy Chalmers bought out of Jack Jarvis's yard on behalf of Ted Sturman (Fred Binns) for £500, who went on to win several good races under both Rules. So it was up to us to change Irian's attitude and help him regain his confidence. He gradually became more amenable, although you would never know what he was going to do and he was quite liable to dig his toes in or make a dart for the gate as he was cantering round the field. We started schooling him as well and that was a bit hit and miss for a while.

Then I gave him a few bits of work but he still didn't show much interest; he would go very well for about three furlongs and then cut out completely. We decided to give him a run anyway and took him to Tralee on 7 November 1978 for the Derrymore Maiden Hurdle—he was jumping the last hurdle when the winner, Lord George, was passing the post!

I rang Raymond and told him we'd give him a couple more runs before condemning him, though I warned Raymond that the horse didn't do much at home either. Irian next ran at Limerick Junction and finished third, beaten over twenty lengths in another maiden hurdle, but the first two, Ardfield and Bright Highway were decent horses. Amazingly, Irian continued to improve by at least seven pounds a fortnight and his attitude at

The Curragh was much better, too. At first, we'd had to gallop him round the field very fast and turn him in quickly over the jumps; now, he loved schooling and Bay Cockburn, a nephew of Fred Rimell's, was getting on with him well, riding him in all his work and in his races.

Irian was next beaten a length and a half by the odds-on favourite Tristram Shandy at Leopardstown on 20 November before running Lord George, who had beaten him so comprehensively first time out, to two and a half lengths at Punchestown on 9 December. Then came his first win, in the Milltown Maiden Hurdle at Leopardstown on 28 December, where he beat Shuilaris by fifteen lengths. He was full of confidence by now, a completely changed horse and Bay never had to hit him, giving him a very good ride into his hurdles which he was jumping better and better all the time.

We kept him in training through the summer of 1979 and, having won a hurdle at Killarney in July, we decided to enter him in the competitive Galway Hurdle on 2 August. He settled in the middle of the field and was staying on steadily at the finish on very fast ground. I felt that if we had him closer to the leaders throughout the race, he might have been in the money. Having slept on it and discussing the race the following day outside the weighing-room with Raymond, I told him he could be a Sweeps Hurdle horse. Irian stayed well, had shown so much on the firm yet loved the soft ground and had always run well at Leopardstown and I knew he would be nicely handicapped.

He won on yielding going at Tralee on 3 September before finishing fifth in the Smithwicks Beer Handicap Hurdle at Listowel on 27 September, but he'd been upset and become excited by a long parade and big crowd that day and ran too free; he'd burned himself out in the race. The same happened when we ran him at Naas on 20 October; he was in very good condition physically but mentally he'd got a bit wound up, having been in training for over a year now, so I told Raymond to take him home for a month and give him a change.

That worked wonders. Irian returned to me on 21 November covered in mud, he'd let down well and was much more relaxed. We started training him again and I thought we might run in one race before Leopardstown; in the end, he missed it and I decided to produce him for the Sweeps without another run. We brought him on to the stage where we took him with a useful hurdler, Jolly Jay, who had won seven races for us, for a racecourse school at Punchestown. My brother-in-law, Tommy Carberry, rode Irian and he beat Jolly Jay at level weights by about fifteen lengths. The work could have been deceptive but we were well pleased, though it put Tommy on the spot because Jim Dreaper had Straight Row in the race and in my heart I couldn't really make out a better case for Irian than Straight Row.

Tommy was prepared to ride Irian but said he would wait and see how Straight Row ran in a condition hurdle at Down Royal the following Wednesday; in the event, Straight Row ran a cracker behind Chinrullah and seemed well handicapped in the Sweeps with 11st 3 lbs.

Tommy, of course, apart from being a top class jockey both on the Flat and over jumps in any country in the world, is a gifted horseman, an excellent work rider, and can give a very accurate account of a horse's ability and potential both on the course and in the horse's gallops. He was an ideal partner for Irian as he was able to transmit his own excellent temperament to the horse and give him confidence. However, he was very undecided which horse to ride after Down Royal and I felt that after Straight Row's good run, I couldn't encourage him to ride Irian and so he took Straight Row.

I then needed someone who could do ten stone, a good experienced pilot and my immediate reaction was to book Sean Treacy, who was free at the time; however, the next morning Bay Cockburn said he'd do the weight, which would have been his lowest ever and, since he'd played such a major part in rehabilitating Irian, I agreed to put him up. That was the Friday and the race was on the following Thursday with Christmas Day in between on the Tuesday. . . . Bay started wasting but by Christmas morning he realised he wasn't going to make it, so I was once again without a jockey and there were only forty-eight hours to go.

I met Dessie Hughes on The Curragh and asked him to ride Irian, but Mick O'Toole had contacted him the previous evening and booked him for Yellow Dean. I arrived at Leopardstown on Boxing Day still without a jockey and only twenty-four hours to go. Jolly Jay ran that day and finished third which naturally encouraged my hopes for Irian—but I still needed a jockey and was getting desperate.

I was coming out of the weighing-room after the fifth race when I saw Ann Ferris, sitting on the table waiting to ride in the bumper—my God, I thought, that's just the person for Irian. Ann's a natural horsewoman, strong, sympathetic and very experienced; she'd ridden for us before and I knew she could do the weight. I booked her there and then. I had in fact ridden a lot of horses for Ann's father, Willie Rooney, a great Northern horseman and among our winners was an Ulster National on Copper Kiln.

I made no contact with Raymond Keogh; he's the ideal owner for he always says not to bother getting in touch. 'I'll read what I want to know in the papers,' he says. I bumped into Mick O'Toole again later that afternoon and he asked if I had got fixed up; I told him I had booked Ann Ferris and he replied, 'Ah, you'll make history tomorrow with the first lady rider to win the Sweeps Hurdle.' Typical Mick'O!

Irian and Ann Ferris (right), take the last hurdle alongside the favourite Twinburn in the 1979 Sweeps Handicap Hurdle at Leopardstown

When we left for the races, my wife, Mary, who understands horses very well and is a tremendous asset to me, was starting to feel the effects of flu. By the next morning, she was quite ill and had to stay in bed. The doctor came and she told him that we would probably win the Sweeps Hurdle now that she wasn't going to be there!

Irian, having been clipped out on the Monday and had his final workout over my hurdles on Boxing Day morning, arrived in the parade ring in very good condition though perhaps a shade burly. Bay Cockburn came into the ring with me and Raymond was quite surprised that Bay was not in his

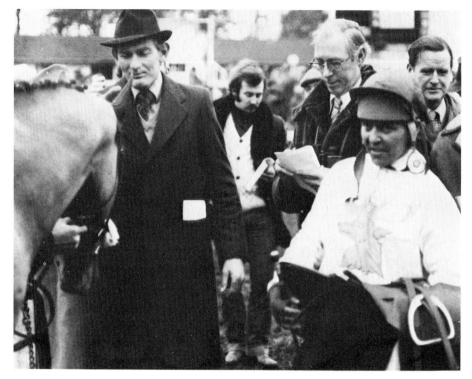

Arthur Moore and Irian after their Sweeps Handicap Hurdle triumph with Ann Ferris

riding gear until we explained he couldn't do the weight. So Raymond asked, 'Who is riding?' 'Ann Ferris,' I replied. 'Ah, that's grand,' said Raymond, 'A lady like.' And then he said, 'Would Irian not have won here yesterday?' I had to admit he'd have had a good chance but I reminded Raymond, who is Master of the Ward Union Staghounds, 'You were hunting yesterday and so you can't go racing on Boxing Day. And anyway,' I told him, 'he won't run so bad here either.' Raymond was still not impressed and turned to his wife, Joan, and enquired, 'Any prizes for coming tenth in this race, Joan? 'You wait and see,' I told him. 'Incidentally, I think you should have a little on him.'

There was an uneasy air about our little group and Ann's arrival did nothing to clear it! She'd never even sat on Irian before, let alone anything else. When I put her up, I told her to keep talking to him and pat him on his neck as he was inclined to get worked up in the parade. In fact, he hardly turned a hair. The instructions were to give him his head, keep him in touch and not to hit him with the stick and make the best of his jumping which by now was a revelation and his strongest point.

Before leaving the ring, I remember looking up at the results board and saw that a horse we thought would run well at Limerick had not even finished in the first three, so I was feeling a bit low as I made my way to the Owners' and Trainers' Stand. Then I bumped into a good friend and owner, in fact our best man, Matty Ryan. He was going to the Tote to have a little each-way on Irian so I told him to double it and we would share the proceeds (Irian paid 90–1 for a win on the Tote.)

The race was a dream. Ann soon had Irian settled, he was in touch all the way down the back straight and closing up at the second last. 'Great,' I thought, 'at least he's run a good race.' He jumped that hurdle terribly well and Ann had him on the inside round the final bend saving invaluable ground. Suddenly, there was just the 6–1 joint favourite, Twinburn, and Irian in it; horses like Chinrullah, Deep Gale, Master Monday and Straight Row weren't going to win. Twinburn jumped the last a bit big but Irian flew it and got away well and then there was that long straight to go, they raced neck and neck . . . photograph! But I had no doubt at all, I knew we'd done it; this gutsy little horse had done it, and with a woman jockey! I raced down the stairs three at a time and was in the winner's enclosure long before Irian was announced the short head winner. Raymond couldn't believe it, he was in the clouds; it was a terrific thrill for us all. Ann, who rode a beautiful race, was quite speechless.

We went home but unfortunately Mary was still feeling quite ill and wasn't able to come out with us to celebrate. However, my parents and a group of friends came out. My father, who hadn't been well for some time and hadn't been racing, was in very good form and thoroughly enjoyed the anecdotes. Sadly, it was the last night he was out socially before his death, as he fell the following day and broke his hip. It was terrific that he was able to share Irian's triumph with us as I had shared so many marvellous moments with him.

# SIR NOEL MURLESS

The record books show that in forty-two years as a trainer, I saddled 1,431 winners, including a record-equalling nineteen English Classic victories—three Derbys, five Oaks, six One Thousand Guineas, two Two Thousand Guineas and three St Legers—five Eclipse Stakes, five Coronation Cups, three King George VI and Queen Elizabeth Stakes and one Ascot Gold Cup.

And I have no hesitation in naming that Ascot Gold Cup victory in 1963 by the four-year-old Twilight Alley as the most memorable performance of any horse I trained. He won it on only his third appearance on the racecourse—a splendid achievement. Yet there had been times when I almost despaired of even running him, let alone winning one of the most prestigous races in the calendar. For there were problems with Twilight Alley right from the day I first set eyes on him . . .

Twilight Alley was out of the Grand Mieuxce mare Crepuscule, who was the dam of my 1957 Derby winner Crepello and also Honeylight, who won the 1956 One Thousand Guineas. I managed Sir Victor Sassoon's stud as well as trained his horses and the usual procedure was that we selected the foals and mares at Newmarket and then I picked out the foals which I thought I'd train.

Luckily I happened to be at The Cliff Stud in Helmsley, on the Yorkshire Moors, when Crepuscule and the foal Twilight Alley by Alycidon arrived from Ireland where Crepuscule had been covered by Hugh Lupus, who won the Irish Two Thousand Guineas and Champion Stakes. I could see straight away that the foal was in a very bad condition with pneumonia and sent for our vet, John Burkhart of Thirsk.

He confirmed the foal was chock full of pneumonia and said he would be lucky to last forty-eight hours. But he picked up remarkably after John pumped him full of antibiotics and gradually began to develop so that we were able to wean him in the normal way. Even so, he was so weak and lanky as a yearling that I didn't bring him into training at Warren Place in

Sir Noel Murless, left,
at Royal Ascot.

Newmarket and left him in Yorkshire until the July of his two-year-old
career.

I just broke him quietly, then gave him little canters and cantering
upsides—but he was virtually a year behind the rest, of course; he was two
and the others were only one!

Twilight Alley went along quietly through the winter and we started to do
a bit of work with him in the spring of 1962; but he showed me nothing. In
the end, I felt I'd better try and get a race into him and selected the
Cranbourn Chase Stakes over 1½ miles at Ascot on 20 July. There were
eleven runners and Bill Rickaby rode him—to our surprise, he won by a very
comfortable two lengths.

Bill always had Twilight Alley in a handy position, though six furlongs
out, four lengths would have covered the entire field. Twilight Alley seemed
to be slightly interfered with just before going into the bend but he made
light of it and passed six horses in the first 200 yards up the straight before
taking the lead with 300 yards to go.

Twilight Alley was already bigger than Crepello, a full 17.1 hands, and I
was so thrilled with the chestnut that I told the *Sporting Life*'s correspondent Tom Nickalls, 'This colt will win the Gold Cup next year!'

I had fitted Twilight Alley, like Crepello, with cloth boots that day just as a precautionary measure—but I was not prepared for the big shock shortly after the race. Sir Victor, alas, had died before Twilight Alley's sparkling debut but Lady Sassoon, like her husband, always liked to have her good horses insured. The Newmarket vet came up and checked him over—and then dropped a bombshell: 'This horse has a murmur in his heart,' he reported.

There was no way I could have him insured under the circumstances—and I decided to put him away and not run him again that year. I never kept my horses cantering through the winter—I always stopped them. Then I'd start them trotting in January and cantering in February. I liked to break their routine and cut their feed before they started to do any fast work at all. I found that horses trained at Newmarket needed more work than those trained on downland.

But Twilight Alley continued to be an enigma at home. He was worse than ever on the gallops when we started working him again; he still wouldn't show anything at all. I'd always had the 1963 Gold Cup in mind for him of course but the weeks were ticking by; he'd only had the one race and it was 3 June before I ran him again—in the Henry II Stakes over 2 miles at Sandown. The Gold Cup was then just seventeen days away.

Lester Piggot rode Twilight Alley this time and they finished second to Lord Sefton's Gaul, beaten one length and a half. Twilight Alley was getting 8 lbs from Gaul but I was pleased with him and I later learned, as they were pulling up, Lester turned to Geoff Lewis, who was on Gaul, and said, 'You know you won't win any Gold Cup.' Geoff replied, 'Well, what's going to beat me?' and Lester said, 'I'll beat you!'

For all that, I still felt I hadn't found the key to Twilight Alley. He was a lovely actioned horse, a beautiful mover but he still wouldn't put it in at home. It didn't matter where I took him; indeed, I think he did less on the Racecourse side than on the Bury side. Yet he had a marvellous temperament; he was like a great big dog, a bit of a pet, and he'd become a great favourite in the yard.

On returning to Warren Place from Sandown, I decided to seek some advice from Doug Smith, who had ridden Alycidon to his Gold Cup victory. I asked him how they trained him and he said they just worked him seven furlongs up the Limekilns with a horse each side of him just at his girths. They found it was the only way they could get the horse to work. I decided to do the same with Twilight Alley for the next fortnight—six times in all, getting him to go as sharp as I could; and that was the only preparation I could give him. I knew by then that if I'd taken him to work one and a half miles, he'd have been a furlong behind.

*Opposite page*
Out in front . . .
Lester Piggott and
Twilight Alley
leading the 1963
Ascot Gold Cup field

A golden pair . . . Lester Piggott and Twilight Alley. 'A splendid achievement for any horse to win the Gold Cup on just his third outing,' said Sir Noel Murless

So I was no more than hopeful when we went to the Royal meeting on 20 June for this supreme test over 2½ miles. To tell the truth, I rather expected Twilight Alley to blow up when he came into the straight. There were seven runners but it was a strong field including the previous year's winner, Balto.

Nobody but Lester would have ridden the race he did—he jumped Twilight Alley off in front and stayed there! He dictated a moderate pace from the start and the first four furlongs were little more than a steady canter but Twilight Alley shook off the favourite, Taine, and Monterrico turning into the straight by just lengthening his stride. And when Misti IV came at him with a desperate challenge in the last furlong, Lester picked up our big baby—and that's all he was still—and quickened as only a class horse can. Twilight Alley drew away again to win by a length. Gaul and Geoff Lewis, after moving up to dispute second place with Taine five furlongs out, soon dropped back and finished next to last. Lester was right again!

It was a particularly sweet journey home to Warren Place. I loved Royal Ascot because that's where you see the best horses and, naturally, I loved to have a winner there. But Twilight Alley's victory was something special because there were times when I had begun to doubt him; I'd begun to think that perhaps, after all, he wasn't any good. But I was always a great believer in patience with horses and, bred the way he was, I had to persevere with Twilight Alley. If I had any secret, it may be that I let the horses guide me. I always saw them as flesh and blood—not machines. Even so, it was a splendid achievement for any horse to win the Gold Cup on just his third outing.

Maybe there was just a little more spring in my step as I went round the yard that night. There were no celebrations, I always went straight home after racing no matter what; I've never been what you might call a racing person. I used to get to the racecourse in time to see my horses run and when they were finished I liked to get off home. I liked to get back to Warren Place and the horses; it was always the same, whether it was the Derby or whatever. It was the breeding, the care, the judgement of horses which fascinated me; I always hated anyone else touching my horses' legs and in any case there was always so much to do—there was always tomorrow.

Sadly, there were not many tomorrows for Twilight Alley. He ran just once more—in the King George VI and Queen Elizabeth Stakes at Ascot on 20 July; he was going really well turning into the straight but he split a pastern and Lester had to pull him up in the last furlong. He went to stud but, like all Gold Cup winners, he didn't get much support from breeders.

Hundreds of horses passed through my hands from the day I began training with a string of three in 1935 but Twilight Alley made an indelible impression on me; by the time I retired in 1976, I had been leading trainer nine times but Twilight Alley was surely my most remarkable champion of all.

# VINCENT O'BRIEN

Royal Tan, the middle leg of my Grand National treble—begun by Early Mist in 1953 and completed by Quare Times in 1955—holds a special affection for me of all the winners I have trained since my first runner, Good Days, won at Limerick Junction in May 1944.

If ever a horse deserved to win the National, then Royal Tan surely did; and few victories have given me greater pleasure than his triumph at Aintree on Saturday, 27 March 1954. Twice before he had been denied victory; first, in 1951, when he nearly came down at the last fence and went on to finish second to Nickel Coin and again a year later when he made his only mistake at the last and fell while lying close up to Teal and Legal Joy. He missed the 1953 National because of leg trouble and his victory at Aintree in 1954 was his first for over two years!

Royal Tan was bred by James Toppin at Tullamaine in Tipperary, near Ballydoyle, and first trained by Tim Hyde who took him over as a weak, unbroken three-year-old. Tim soon found he was a natural jumper and hunted him as a four-year-old. I had an owner in my stable, Mrs Moya Keogh, whose horse Hatton's Grace had won the Champion Hurdle in three successive years (1949, 1950 and 1951). In the summer of 1949 I suggested she buy Royal Tan. Royal Tan's sire Tartan, half-brother by Ellangowan to Blue Peter, was bred by Lord Rosebery for whom he had won the Brittania Stakes at Ascot and four other races before the war; he sired a number of good jumping winners.

We won our first race with Royal Tan on 18 February 1950 when, as a six-year-old, he won the 2-mile Milltown Novices Chase at Leopardstown. He had pleased me from the start and we felt he was capable of putting up a good show at Cheltenham eighteen days later but he fell at the second in the National Hunt Chase. He over jumped, became unbalanced and went over. Royal Tan ran twice more that season winding up with a victory in the Maiden Chase at Fairyhouse.

Vincent O'Brien at
home at Ballydoyle
with Royal Tan

We started him off the following October at Leopardstown where he was third of eight in the Johnstown Handicap Chase and he returned there on 11 November to win the Dodder Handicap. Royal Tan jumped well and ran on to finish third in the Kerrymount Handicap at Leopardstown on 13 January 1951 before finishing unplaced in the Leopardstown Chase on 17 February.

Victory in the Kilcoole Handicap Chase at Leopardstown followed by a second in the Irish Grand National at Fairyhouse on 26 March, twelve days before his first crack at Aintree, left us with some optimism for Liverpool and Royal Tan started at 22–1 in a field of thirty-six.

There was more drama than usual even for the 1951 National as there was a bad start and at least twenty of the runners were left. There was chaos at the first fence where twelve either fell or were brought down, and only half a dozen were standing as they reached the fence before the Chair where Russian Hero was baulked and brought down. Gay Heather fell at Becher's second time leaving the mare, Nickel Coin, in front and I could see Royal Tan, with his white blaze, going smoothly on the outside; I always suggested that my jockeys went on the outside in the National, their chance of escaping trouble from loose horses was better there for the fallers invariably went towards the inside where there were no rails and naturally veered that way to avoid jumping the fences in front of them.

Derrinstown, brought down by Gay Heather, was remounted but Broomfield went at the fence after Becher's so it was a two-horse race between Royal Tan and Nickel Coin, a 40–1 outsider trained at Reigate in Surrey by Jack O'Donoghue. Royal Tan looked sure to win coming to the last but made a really bad mistake, hitting the top of the fence and my brother 'Phonsie', by an extraordinary feat of jockeyship, remained on board. Nickel Coin and Johnny Bullock were gone beyond recall and strode away from Royal Tan to win by six lengths with Derrinstown a long way back in third, the only three to survive.

That was naturally a great disappointment and after winning the 3-mile Cowley Novices' Hurdle at Cheltenham the following season, Royal Tan was sold in November 1951 by Mrs Keogh to a young Dublin businessman, Joe Griffin, or 'Mincemeat Joe' as he was known in the Irish canning trade where he had a prospering business. Royal Tan won for the first time in Mr Griffin's colours at the Cheltenham Festival meeting on 5 March, taking the 3-mile National Hunt Handicap Chase in fine style.

So for another crack at the National—although, if Royal Tan had had his way, I doubt whether he'd have left Ireland. Horses have long memories and a certain amount of reasoning power and, when Royal Tan arrived at Waterford to board the boat for Fishguard, no amount of pushing and shoving would move him. We got him on eventually—then he didn't want

'Phonsie' O'Brien pops Royal Tan over a hurdle at Ballydoyle. 'Phonsie came up with the answer to Royal Tan,' said Vincent O'Brien

to get off the boat at the other end and we very nearly missed the train to Liverpool!

He seemed all right on the day, however, and Phonsie, who had won on him at Cheltenham, had the ride. There was again chaos at the first fence with ten of the forty-seven runners departing. Royal Tan and Phonsie survived all the drama and they came to the last full of running, behind Legal Joy and Teal. Again Royal Tan blundered and this time fell—my National hopes were shattered once more.

Most distressing of all, Royal Tan developed tendon trouble in 1952. This necessitated a long rest and he did not race again until October 1953. As a side effect of this prolonged and enforced lay-off, Royal Tan had become more than usually lazy.

However, I won my first National in 1953 with Early Mist, whom I bought a year earlier for Joe Griffin for 5,300 guineas at the J. V. Rank dispersal sale.

Royal Tan resumed chasing on 31 October 1953 in the 3-mile Blessington Handicap at Naas and Bryan Marshall, whom we retained, came over from England to ride him for the first time. Royal Tan carried 12st 7 lbs and was unplaced but at least he was sound afterwards.

We followed that with a run over hurdles at Leopardstown on 9 January and Bryan rode again; Royal Tan was among the outsiders and again unplaced. I was happy enough with him, however, and like all my jumping horses, I schooled him twice a week as part of his training schedule to keep the jumping muscles in trim and his mental processes alert. Royal Tan, without doubt was the best natural jumper I trained and I was very perplexed when Bryan parted company with him at the open ditch in the Thyestes Handicap at Gowran Park on 21 January.

It seemed the horse and rider were not getting on together, and it was Phonsie who came up with the answer. He felt Royal Tan was such a good and natural jumper that he didn't want a jockey dictating to him. Where Bryan had been able to gather up Early Mist and present him at his fences, Royal Tan had to be left to jump exactly as he wished. The jockey had to sit still and leave it to the horse. Probably Royal Tan's two errors at the last fence in earlier Nationals had been due to a very understandable anxiety on Phonsie's part to get the horse over the last obstacle.

Bryan returned to Ireland to ride the horse in a school over fences at Gowran Park and rode him as Phonsie suggested; he came back smiling, confident that we'd found the answer to the problem. This was only a few weeks before the National so it was a great stroke of luck that we found out in time what was wrong.

I ran two other horses in the 1954 National, Alberoni and Churchtown. Royal Tan, backed down from 100–7 in the three weeks before the race, was the 8–1 second favourite in the twenty-nine-horse field; he'd carried 10st 13 lbs in 1951 and 11st 6 lbs in 1952 and this time had top weight of 11st 7 lbs.

In view of Royal Tan's reluctance to travel two years earlier, I decided not to take him straight to Liverpool; instead, we installed him twenty miles away at Haydock Park. I thought it might revive memories of Liverpool if he went straight to the racecourse stables with my other runners for Aintree, so he went with Christie Tuchy to the quiet and seclusion of Haydock and they made the short trip to the racecourse on the morning of the race.

Alberoni fell at the first and almost brought Royal Tan down; however, luck was with us. Royal Tan jumped very well and Bryan had him racing nicely first time around. Approaching the third fence from home, Churchtown looked to have the better chance. He headed the leader, but hit the second last fence hard and almost came down losing vital lengths.

Royal Tan and Bryan Marshall were tracking Tudor Line and going easily, but I was very apprehensive as Royal Tan came to the last fence, and I wondered if the horse would throw the race away—or would it be third time lucky? He had passed Tudor Line between the last two and Bryan sat

still over the last as we had agreed; the horse jumped perfectly and they were over and racing for home. Tudor Line, who had a special bit to stop him jumping to the right, still jumped right but George Slack got Tudor Line to run for his life. They slowly, relentlessly, closed the gap but Royal Tan was equal to him and these two magnificent chestnuts and their riders gave everything in a pulsating finish up that never-ending last quarter of a mile; still Tudor Line kept coming, but still Royal Tan ran on—and held on by just a neck. Who could deny him that victory after all the disappointment.

It had been sixty-nine years since a jockey had ridden the National winner in consecutive years, Mr E. P. Wilson having won on Voluptuary (1884) and Roquefort (1885); and the last occasion an owner had won in successive years with different horses was 1912 and 1913 when Sir Charles Assheton-Smith won with Jerry M. and Covertcoat.

For my part, it was a great, great thrill; Joe Griffin gave a party at Liverpool afterwards and we came back to Ireland to a Civic reception in Dublin where Royal Tan was received by the Lord Mayor and paraded through the streets. There were bonfires everywhere and, when we returned to Ballydoyle, The Rock of Cashel was lit up as we completed our journey. It was quite something then for the Irish to win the National, and to win it two

Bryan Marshall and Royal Tan avoid the fallen Alberoni at the first fence in the 1954 Grand National years in a row, was very special; but to go on and make it a hat-trick in 1955, well, that's another story . . .

Royal Tan, for all his dislike of Aintree—and make no mistake, he hated the place—returned to finish twelfth in 1955 and third behind E.S.B. in 1956 before being carried out at Becher's on the first circuit in 1957, his last race. Prince Aly Khan, who had bought Royal Tan when Joe Griffin was declared bankrupt in the autumn of 1954, gave him to the Duchess of Devonshire and he spent a peaceful, happy retirement roaming the grounds at Lismore Castle.

# MICK O'TOOLE

There are milestones in a man's life which, once achieved, are savoured and remembered with warmth and gratitude for ever. Such a moment for me was Davy Lad's victory in the 2½-mile Sun Alliance Novices' Hurdle at the Cheltenham Festival of 1975 and not even the memory of the atrocious weather that day will ever dampen the joy of satisfaction and relief I felt when Davy Lad and Dessie Hughes returned in triumph to the hallowed crescent of grass outside the weighing-room—my first winner at the festival.

I'll never forget the moment when Davy Lad, a magnificent, brown gelding, beat the Queen Mother's Sunyboy by three lengths with Express Mail a head away third and Aldaniti, who was to become the Aintree hero of 1981, fifteen lengths back in fourth.

If Davy Lad had never won again, he would have held a special place in my heart and memory, though two years later he was to produce the battling qualities he showed that day when he won the Cheltenham Gold Cup. But Thursday, 13 March 1975 marked the end of a very important chapter in my life and set me in search of horses to re-live, annually if possible, the glow and emotion which a victory at Cheltenham means to most Irishmen.

Yet I only came across Davy Lad by accident at the old Ballsbridge Sales in May 1973. I called into the Sales after running a friend to Dublin Airport. I had nothing special in mind but was immediately taken by Davy Lad; he was quite simply the nicest horse on view and he had a certain character and outlook which caught you as soon as you came in contact with him. We went to £5,500 for him, a lot for an unbroken three-year-old and took him back to Maddenstown on the edge of The Curragh. That 100-box yard was a far cry from my early days at Phoenix Park where I'd started out with three horses after previously training greyhounds. One of my uncles, Willie Byrne, trained horses very successfully and another, Paddy Byrne, trained dogs and I never had any intention myself of doing anything except train.

Mick O'Toole...
'Davy Lad holds a
special place in my
heart.'

I bought Davy Lad because I had a particular regard for horses by Pampered King, a horse that Jack Doyle and I both loved. He was the sire of the St Leger third, David Jack, and he in turn was the sire of Davy Lad: that was half the attraction of him. David Jack in time also sired Jack of Trumps and Dramatist, and so proved our hunch that he would make a sire of top class National Hunt horses.

We broke Davy Lad that summer but he was terribly backward and we had to bring him on slowly until he ran in a hurdle at Naas on 26 January 1974; he started at 20–1 and finished second to Tony Redmond's Bilbo Baggins. By then I'd sold him, along with another horse called Arctic Heir, for £15,000 to Anne Marie McGowan, whose husband is in the property business and, for relaxation, he thought it might be nice to have a couple of promising National Hunt horses.

Some people are born lucky and Anne Marie and Joe McGowan must fit into that category when one thinks that their first ever horse won at Cheltenham and then two years later won the Gold Cup. Since then, they've tasted that joy and emotion on two further occasions, with Parkhill and Hartstown.

I like to give horses a run over hurdles first and then, if you want to bring them back after a bumper or two, you don't have to start teaching them again; that's what we did with Davy Lad, and did he win his bumper!

Needless to say, Davy Lad didn't go unsupported when he won his first bumper at Fairyhouse and he was even more impressive next time at Leopardstown where he won the Rogers for Racing Bumper beating a 'hot-pot', Romaunt, who was reputed to be one of the nicest horses Paddy Sleator had had for a very long time.

All Ireland seemed to know about Davy Lad by then and we fancied a pop at Cheltenham's four-year-old championship, the *Daily Express* Triumph Hurdle. After Leopardstown, his price had tumbled from 100–1 to 8–1 second favourite, and that put a certain amount of extra pressure on us. It is not good for racing to disgruntle punters by their losing ante-post wagers, but fools go in where angels etc., and regrettably not only did he not win the *Daily Express* hurdle, he didn't even run. There are many more disappointments with National Hunt horses than people imagine and on this occasion Davy Lad had a kidney infection and Cheltenham had to wait a further year.

Instead he ran at Leopardstown on the Saturday of Cheltenham week, 16 March, and finished second, beaten two lengths by Tall Noble starting at 2–1 on for the 2-mile Windy Arbour Maiden Hurdle; as it turned out, that was the sweetest defeat I ever suffered, for if he had won at Leopardstown he wouldn't have been qualified to run in the Sun Alliance Novices' Hurdle the following year!

Davy Lad did well during the summer and came out fresh to win the 2-mile Ballagh Maiden Hurdle at Galway on 9 September 1974; and then he won the 2-mile Valentia Hurdle at Listowel on 24 September before making it a hat-trick in the Saggart Hurdle at Naas on 12 October. We took him to Punchestown on 23 October where he finished sixth carrying an eight-pound penalty in the 2-mile Free Handicap Hurdle won by Tied Cottage, who was then a six-year-old; seventeen days later, Davy Lad trotted up in the Rossmore Hurdle at Naas.

Then came a real setback; he had a fall one day schooling and hurt a hock, nothing serious it seemed but clearly the horse was very sore. Then, as the weeks went by, he failed to improve and was lame on and off all the time until the New Year. Cheltenham began to seem another planet away and we only made it in the end because of the skill and patience of my vet, Bob Griffin, and Dessie Hughes. Davy Lad didn't work properly again until February and we forgot any idea of running him before Cheltenham; we took him to Leopardstown several times and Dessie rode him in schools with Arctic Heir and Mr Know All but it was touch and go whether we'd get to Cheltenham. However, he was soon working well enough and once again all Ireland seemed to know about it.

Davy Lad arrived safe and sound at Cheltenham but our worries weren't

Davy Lad and Dessie Hughes take the last fence in front in the 1975 Sun Alliance Novices' Hurdle at Cheltenham

over; that was the first of the very bad years weatherwise we had at Cheltenham and by the Thursday, the final day of the meeting, the going was heavy, very heavy. I arrived at the course in the morning fearing that the meeting would be abandoned. When the Stewards did give the all-clear, it was decided to leave out the second last hurdle; that didn't help us, jumping being the name of the game and jumping being very much the name of Davy Lad's game, for he was a brilliant, fluent jumper.

He was often down and sullen but happiest when all around him were uncomfortable. His heart always cheered up when he passed tired horses either in the air or when he galloped past them, and he came 'on the boil' as the strain hurt others.

I had a bet—Davy Lad was never more than his starting price of 5–2 favourite after opening 2–1—and went up to the stands to watch the race with Jack Doyle and Dr Paddy Morrissey, and John Mulhern joined us. Inventory took them along until two out and Dessie sent Davy Lad on at the top of the hill; they jumped the last flight badly to the left but he received all the help Dessie could give him to hold on to his lead on the flat as Sunyboy ran on well—and there was a fair bit of encouragement from the stands, too!

My first Cheltenham winner! Marvellous. We had a few jars that night and then a few more, but that was nothing in comparison with the celebrations after he won the Gold Cup two years later at 14–1. You need luck in this game, and luck was on Davy Lad's side that day and as others around him struggled or fell, his confidence 'brimmed'. He battled through, caught a weary Tied Cottage and ran on up the hill to win by six lengths.

Although I now train as many on the Flat as I do over jumps—and Dickens Hill gave me a marvellous season in 1979 when he was second to Troy in both the Derby and the Irish Derby as well as winning the Irish Two Thousand Guineas and the Eclipse—I'll always retain my love for the jumping game; and for Cheltenham in particular.

# RYAN PRICE

Racing historians will tell you that Persian Lancer became the first eight-year-old to win the Cesarewitch at Newmarket on Saturday, 1 October 1966; that it was jockey Doug Smith's sixth win in the race, the first being back in 1939; and it was my second Cesarewitch with only my second runner, Utrillo having won in 1963. But behind those stark facts lies a tale of despair and heartache, of patience and dedication. If ever a horse deserved to win a big race, then it was Persian Lancer, a bay gelding by Persian Gulf out of Bay Lancer who was by Nearco. I'd never known a horse get so mucked about in his races during my forty-five years as a trainer.

Persian Lancer's early years were full of promise. He was owned as a two-and three-year-old by Greek ship owner Stavros Niarchos and trained by Sir Gordon Richards at Ogbourne Maisey, running four times in 1960 and once finishing second, at Bath. Doug Smith rode him for the first time in his fourth race as a three-year-old when they won the Nearco Handicap over 1 mile 5 furlongs at Sandown on 10 June 1961. Two races later, Persian Lancer, with Scobie Breasley riding, won the Melrose Handicap at York over 1 mile 6 furlongs. Scobie was third on him in the 2-mile Melbourn Handicap at Newmarket on 27 September—seventeen days before Persian Lancer's first crack at the Cesarewitch.

Ironically, Doug chose Persian Lancer for the 1961 Cesarewitch in preference to the four-year-old Avon's Pride who was trained by Major Dick Hern. Avon's Pride, with Doug's brother Eph riding, held on to win by a short head from Alcoa with Persian Lancer a further three-quarters of a length back in third! But that race was to hold a vital key five years later for Doug had taken it up inside the final furlong and time told it was imperative to hold up Persian Lancer until the last possible moment. It was nonetheless an outstanding performance by the three-year-old for the race had been run in a very fast time, three minutes 57.92 seconds, 4.08 seconds under average.

Ryan Price follows in
Doug Smith and
Persian Lancer after
their victory in the
1966 Cesarewitch

Then came the despair and heartache. Persian Lancer broke down badly on his near foreleg soon after the race and Mr Niarchos gave the horse to his racing manager, Lord Belper, who had Persian Lancer on his estate in Nottinghamshire before sending him to Syd Mercer in Oxfordshire to see what could be done. There was even greater anguish to suffer for the horse had an extraordinary accident after getting loose at Syd Mercer's; he ended up under a bus which had to be lifted by tackle to release Persian Lancer.

Somehow he survived that and Lord Belper refused to accept defeat, showing great patience and faith in a horse who undoubtedly had the potential of a top-class stayer. Lord Belper decided to send him to me in 1963 to see if there was any chance of getting him sound. He ran twice that year, finishing unplaced on both occasions at Ascot and Nottingham; then we had him fired and blistered and it was over two years before I could contemplate running him again.

We eventually had him back on the racecourse on 9 December 1965 in a 2-mile novice hurdle at Wincanton with Paul Kelleway riding. The seven-year-old Persian Lancer was unplaced—but at least he was back on the track and he ran five more times over hurdles between then and the following March, once being carried out at Kempton when he was 5–2 favourite and holding every chance two out. He was unplaced in the Imperial Cup Handicap Hurdle at Sandown next time out when I put a hood on him as he had started to show signs of temperament.

Although Persian Lancer hadn't managed a win, I was satisfied in my own mind that he would stand racing and we started him at Kempton in the 1966 Flat season; we fitted blinkers and Eric Eldin rode him but they were unplaced in the 2-mile Queen's Prize on 11 April.

Persian Lancer was unplaced in a 2-mile race at Lingfield the following month—without blinkers—but we put the blinds on again at Bath on 11 June for the 2-mile 1 furlong Clevedon Handicap. Scobie Breasley rode him this time but he didn't act on the track and after hitting the front too soon, finished second, beaten two and a half lengths by Party Choice. Seven days later, we went to Ascot for the 2-mile Halifax Stakes and he was beaten half a length by All Found, giving the winner 10 lbs. This was a significant race, however, for Jock Wilson held him up for a late run and both the tactics and the track clearly suited him.

He failed to act at Chester the following month and finished third in the 2-mile 2-furlong Greenall Whitley Gold Trophy, before going to Good-wood on 27 July for the Goodwood Stakes Handicap over 2-miles 3 furlongs. The apprentice Fred Messer, who had ridden Persian Lancer at Chester, rode him again and the horse was well fancied, being backed from 8–1 to 11–2 second favourite to Square Deal. Persian Lancer made head-

way four furlongs out, led inside the final furlong, and was beaten a neck by
All Found. He'd once again hit the front too soon but I was convinced after
this that he could win the Cesarewitch even then at the age of eight and
despite all the problems. With that in mind, I gave him a break from racing
and set about preparing him for Newmarket. Persian Lancer was always a
good doer and we kept him fit with regular roadwork; we couldn't
overwork him at Findon for fear of his breaking down.

I was delighted when the weights were published for the Cesarewitch—
Persian Lancer was given 7st 6 lbs, the same as he had carried in the 1961
race. Doug Smith had put up 2 lbs overweight then and I knew he'd have to
do the same again but he was the man for the job. But Doug hadn't ridden
the horse since the 1961 Cesarewitch and wanted to renew his association,
so Doug was on board for the 2-mile Florizel Handicap at Kempton on 17
September. Persian Lancer was made 100–30 favourite but finished fourth;
he was well behind for twelve furlongs, made rapid headway three out,
challenged over a furlong out, and ran on at one pace. Doug admitted he
had gone too soon; he knew now for sure that the horse had to be held for
the last possible moment.

Nonetheless, it was the perfect trial and I was confident that the horse
would win the Cesarewitch. He should have trotted up on more than one
occasion but he'd been desperately unlucky. He was now a much stronger
horse than when he'd finished third as a three-year-old and I had no doubt
that this was his course and distance; plenty of others shared my view for he
was backed from 33–1 to 100–7.

There had been a dry spell just prior to the race but the rain lashed down
the day before taking the sting out of the ground. I had one minor
worry—Doug's fitness. He had missed the previous two days' racing with a
torn chest muscle but he exercised Persian Lancer on the morning of the race
and declared himself fit. I had no doubt about Persian Lancer—he was spot
on, 100 per cent; and I wasn't worried about Doug putting up that 2 lbs
overweight, his knowledge of the horse was vital.

On paper, the race looked competitive. Mintmaster, the previous year's
winner, and Miss Dawn, winner of her three previous races, had dominated
the ante-post market along with Persian Lancer. The field of twenty-four
also included the Ascot Stakes' winner Tubalcain and Persian Lancer's
Ascot and Goodwood conqueror, All Found. It may have looked a hot race
before but I've never seen an easier winner!

It was a grey day and the first mile was obscured by mist. Doug had
Persian Lancer well behind in the early stages—I had told him I'd crucify
him if he hit the front any sooner than the winning post! As the field
approached The Bushes, only the 66–1 outsider C.E.D. and Miss Dawn,

Ryan Price and Persian Lancer, sixteen years after his Cesarewitch triumph. 'He's enjoying his retirement, whiling away the hours quietly on my Downs at home,' said Ryan Price

who had set a blistering pace, were in front of Persian Lancer. It was surprising that so many horses who had shown ample stamina on other courses should be so hopelessly beaten so far out. This was now the worrying time; I could see Doug going so easily that he was in great danger of having to go on. The tiring C.E.D. swerved sharply across the track and back and Doug had to corkscrew to keep on his tail, but with a hundred yards to go, he thrust for home, led fifty yards out and won as he liked by three-quarters of a length from C.E.D. with Miss Dawn eight lengths away third.

Ronnie Belper couldn't help teasing Doug as he and Persian Lancer were led in: 'Always knew you couldn't obey riding instructions.' 'I couldn't help it,' replied Doug. 'The horse was going far too well too far from home. How could I keep him tucked in behind when I knew half a mile out he just had to win?'

I think the satisfaction I had from this result surpassed all the training successes I've been lucky to have for it reflected years of patience on the part of Persian Lancer's owner, great dedication on the part of my veterinarians and staff and a vindication of my belief that the horse could win the Cesarewitch from some considerable time before. The horse, a cripple, and without a win of any kind for five seasons, more than deserved his triumph on the day for we had spent three years fiddling with that near foreleg and only had him right that season. Now, I'm delighted to say, he's enjoying his retirement, whiling away the hours quietly on my Downs at home.

# FRED RIMELL

Fred Rimell was interviewed on 13 May 1981, and returned his approved chapter the day before his untimely death.

Four Grand Nationals in twenty-one years—the first man to train four National winners, and to think I'd always regarded Liverpool as something of a jinx course in my riding days! It's a funny thing really, for although I rode quite a lot of winners, I never got one home at Aintree over hurdles or fences—and I was even pipped a neck on the Flat on a horse called Promptitude in the 1928 Liverpool Spring Cup.

But that's another story. My story, my Greatest Triumph, has to be that quartet of National winners—ESB in 1956, Nicolaus Silver (1961), Gay Trip (1970) and Rag Trade in 1976.

A story which began with one of the most dramatic Grand Nationals of all time and centred around a super horse called ESB, who Mercy and I first saw as an unbroken three-year-old in a field near Lapworth in Warwickshire. He was by the French sire Bidar out of English Summer—hence his initialled name—and as soon as we set eyes on him, a lovely dark bay, we fell in love with him. He had been bred in Ireland and bought as a youngster by his then owner Mr Blackstead from whom we bought him for £1,750 on behalf of Rowley Oliver.

He was that wonderful rich, genuine colour, with a quality head, good big ears and a bold eye. He had great depth through the heart, a fine spring of rib, powerful quarters and a good straight hind leg with a strong second thigh. He gave the impression of power, quality and balance.

As soon as we had broken him, we taught him to gallop and he took naturally to jumping. He was not a difficult horse to train; we had to run him in blinkers two or three times just to make him go and do his job but he really was a very bold horse. I trained him in his first four seasons, then he had a season each with Syd Mercer and Leonard Carver before returning to me. Funnily enough, the Carvers who had now bought him, owned the land adjoining the field in which we had first seen ESB—they had been looking at him over the hedge since he was a yearling and did nothing about him!

He began the 1955–56 season running down the field in a hurdle race at Worcester and then won a Handicap Chase at Birmingham before finishing second to Irish Lizard in the Christmas Cracker Handicap Chase at Liverpool at the end of November 1955. After that, he went to Warwick and won the 3-mile Hatton Handicap Chase, finished third in another 3-mile Handicap Chase there, and then won the 3½-mile Tom Coulthwaite Handicap Chase at Haydock which provided experience over some drop fences—nothing like as big as the drops at Liverpool, but nevertheless helpful to a horse to understand that the landing may be lower than the take-off.

Then we took on Sundew in the Hearts of Oak Handicap at Manchester in March. ESB received 6 lbs from Sundew who led to the last fence where ESB took it up and went on to win by one and a half lengths. That was good form and gave us quiet confidence for Liverpool.

I had learned to regard the National as just another race because I had had so many disappointments at Aintree. All the nervous tension which builds up in the minds of owners, trainers and particularly jockeys before the National is communicated to the horse, but I had the ideal animal for the job in ESB, then ten years old and a winner of eighteen races.

In the old days when the fences were straight, the horses used to get underneath them when they tired and could not afford to get too close and make mistakes. They were very stiff. They have altered so much in recent years and now this beautiful apron has brought the fences out. They run up the fences more and are certainly easier to jump than they were in ESB's year.

I engaged Dave Dick a fine, brave long-legged rider, because Tim Molony, my stable jockey, was committed to my old friend, Willie Stephenson. An estimated quarter of a million people were at Aintree and many, naturally, were hoping for a Royal victory for the Queen Mother and her big, quality bay chaser, Devon Loch.

Devon Loch put up a magnificent display of jumping but Dave Dick gave our horse a super ride. He got into a bit of trouble at the fence after the Canal Turn on the final circuit and another horse almost brought him down.

He gradually made up all his ground and arrived at the last upsides Devon Loch. But Devon Loch ran us out of it on the flat and I resolved to be second—another disappointment at Liverpool.

Then suddenly about fifty yards from the post, Devon Loch seemed to go to jump at something that wasn't there and slithered along the ground. He came to a complete stop with his forefeet stretched in front of him and his hind legs lagging in the rear.

Dave Dick, who had just dropped his hands accepting inevitable defeat, reacted quickly, picked ESB up and drove him past the post ten lengths clear from Gentle Moya and Royal Tan.

It was a funny feeling really because, as I walked off the stand, I was saying to myself, 'Good God, what a terrible thing to happen to anybody, the way that horse collapsed—Christ, I've won a bloody National!' I could hardly believe it and then it suddenly all dawned on me.

Yet, when I looked at the film afterwards, I think we would have been unlucky losers because ESB was badly interfered with and had so much ground to make up after the Canal Turn. A horse fell in front of him and very nearly brought him down. He still arrived at the last upsides Devon Loch but had taken an awful lot out of himself doing it, whereas Dick Francis on Devon Loch had a beautiful ride throughout and I don't think he was interfered with at all.

We went up with Mr and Mrs Carver to be presented to the Queen and the Queen Mother, who showed no sign of the disappointment she must

Dave Dick salutes ESB's triumph in the 1956 Grand National . . . and Fred Rimell's record-breaking run in the race has just begun

have felt. I talked with the Queen Mother and said what a terrible thing it was to happen but she just brushed it aside and said, 'Well, Mr Rimell, you have won a National.'

I think she is the most wonderful person we have had in racing. I doubt whether we would have had jumping at Ascot without her asking for it—she has been the most wonderful supporter that National Hunt racing could have had. And fifteen years later, when she was presenting me with my fourth successive Mackeson Gold Cup following Gay Trip's second win in three years in the race, she smiled at me and said, 'This is becoming a habit, Mr Rimell.' She's a wonderful lady.

That, then, was ESB, the horse who changed my Liverpool luck. Somehow, I felt 24 March 1956 was going to be my day from the moment I collected the No. 7 cloth—my lucky number—and Dave Dick came into the ring wearing the Carver's green and white—I regard green as my lucky colour. Not that I'm particularly superstitious . . .

Then there was Silver! Nicolaus Silver, a most beautiful jumper, a superb-looking horse who would have won any lightweight show class. A perfect mover who could never have been beaten in the show ring—he was the nicest of my National winners.

I had an owner, Jeremy Vaughan, who had been pestering me for a long time to find him a National horse. I rang him one day and told him there were two horses to see at Ballsbridge in Dublin—My Flame and Nicolaus Silver. Jeremy came over with us and we made straight for the two horses Mercy had picked out of the catalogue. My Flame was out of the question—far too small, a pony. But Nicolaus Silver was gorgeous.

Every horse had to qualify to run in the National by winning a race of certain value: fortunately the catalogue did not show that Nicolaus Silver was already qualified—Mercy, though, had checked and realised he was. If others had known that this lovely quality grey horse was qualified for Aintree, I am sure we would not have been able to buy him. Ivor Herbert was the underbidder to us—and we got him for 2,600 guineas.

We were delighted. He was a horse that loved very good ground. The first time we ran him, on 7 January 1961, it was dreadfully heavy at Windsor. He finished second over 3 miles and Tim Brookshaw got off and said, 'This horse will win a National for you.'

We ran him three times after that before he went to Cheltenham and won the Kim Muir Memorial Challenge Cup and he jumped with a precision that gave us confidence for Aintree. Stan Mellor and Tim Brookshaw, the two jockeys we were using at the time, had committed themselves to other trainers so we engaged Bobby Beasley, the young Irish champion jockey.

Jeremy Vaughan was on holiday in Spain when I gave Nicolaus his last serious piece of work with two horses, one to take him a mile and a half and the other to jump in and take him the last half-mile. They were useful animals but he thrashed the pair of them. We sent Jeremy the news and at that time, the price was about 66–1—I'm happy to say he stood to win a lot of money over the horse.

Although the Irish horse Jonjo was backed at the last moment from 100–7 to 7–1 favourite, the obvious danger was the previous year's winner Merryman II, a massive, old-fashioned sort who was more than capable of carrying top weight of 11st 12 lbs. I very much doubted, though, whether even he, grand individual that he was, could give 25 lbs to Nicolaus Silver over four and a half miles.

As they walked up to the tapes, Merryman was kicked by Jimuru and led out of the line, but after inspection it was rightly decided that all was well. Merryman showed no ill effects and went on to run a tremendous race.

Fresh Winds had a long lead as they came on to the racecourse for the first time ahead of Imposant with Merryman third and Nicolaus Silver in the bunch behind, really enjoying himself—galloping and jumping splendidly.

Nicolaus made his only mistake at Becher's second time and Bobby said afterwards, 'He was on his nose.' Merryman was going really well in the lead by then, jumping boldly, accurately and fast with no sign of weakening. When Fresh Winds fell at the nineteenth, Merryman was left in front of Nicolaus, Wyndburgh, O'Malley Point, Scottish Flight II and Kilmore. They were well clear of the rest.

As they rounded the Canal Turn, we could see that Bobby was sitting with a double handful on our horse who was still going well within himself. Bobby brought Nicolaus up on Merryman's outside to launch his final challenge as they came to the last. He was going so easily with Merryman desperately trying to keep on terms. Bobby kept our horse going strongly and the grey ran on to win in magnificent style.

Derek Ancil and Merryman fought all the way but Nicolaus ran home with his ears pricked, a most impressive winner by five lengths in 9 minutes 22 3/5 seconds—the fastest since the victory of ESB and only 2 1/5 seconds slower than Golden Miller's record in 1934.

No grey horse had won the National for ninety years and Jeremy Vaughan couldn't believe it. Mercy and I were not grumbling either. We had a nice each-way bet at 45–1. I always thought Nicolaus was a Liverpool horse because he was such a clean jumper. He would give a fence three or four inches or a foot if he thought he could, and I think I got more thrill out of him than any of the others.

*Opposite page*
Nicolaus Silver and
Bobby Beasley on
their way to victory
in the 1961 National

\*      \*      \*

The first time I set eyes on Gay Trip, I was amazed—he had four huge legs like bolsters. His owner had blistered him all round! Pat Taaffe had recommended Gay Trip at a time when we were looking for a horse for our old hunting friend, Tony Chambers. When I arrived at the place near Naas to see Gay Trip, he had been turned out into a field. Of course, I was a bit annoyed to think I'd gone all that way to see a horse which was blistered. But I returned with Tony a few weeks later; the legs had fined down, the price was right and we knew that this was just what we had been looking for.

He was a little bay Vulgan horse—a slight horse, only just sixteen hands and not all that robust. But he turned out to be a machine—a very athletic horse, an extremely good jumper and very brainy.

The first time he ran for us—in the Halloween Novices' Chase at Newbury in October 1967—we had quite a few quid on him and he fell at the water in front of the stands. Of course, they never jump the water in Ireland—he just put his toe in the edge and turned over. But we went to Doncaster for a 2½-mile Novices' Chase a month later and had a nice touch on him and he won very convincingly.

He won his first Mackeson Gold Cup in 1969 helping to prove my theory that a 2½-mile horse is suitable for the 4½-mile Grand National. I always feel that a 2½-mile horse has enough speed to get out of trouble at Liverpool and if he is a good enough jumper he will reserve himself; that I think is the ideal animal for Aintree.

Gay Trip was second in the Massey Ferguson and fourth in the King George VI Chase at Kempton behind Titus Oates, before going to the Festival where he was sixth behind L'Escargot in the Gold Cup. We were delighted. This was great preparation for the National in sixteen days' time.

But there was sadness before the race—our jockey Terry Biddlecombe had fractured three ribs and damaged a kidney in a fall at Kempton in the February so we turned to Pat Taaffe, who had originally recommended Gay Trip to us, for the Aintree mount. He had top weight of 11st 5 lbs—six lbs more than any other runner in the twenty-eight horse field—but outclassed them over the last two miles.

He seemed to be pulling double and going best of all as they passed the stands the first time round when he was sixth. Villay was leading from Miss Hunter, Assad, The Otter, No Justice, Dozo and Gay Trip with Pat giving him a glorious ride. Villay unseated his rider at the 27th, and Vulture and Dozo were in front with Gay Trip going so easily and smoothly just behind.

Then a match developed between Dozo and Gay Trip and, coming back on to the racecourse, Dozo began to run out of stamina and we knew then that Pat was going to win. Gay Trip jumped like a machine and went further

away from the rest, winning handsomely in the end by twenty lengths from Vulture with Miss Hunter third.

I had always favoured Gay Trip's chance in preference to my other runner, French Excuse, the ante-post favourite, who in fact fell at the Canal Turn first time round. Gay Trip was a marvellous animal though a little highly-strung—that is, until he developed a friendship with a Nanny goat called Minnie, who travelled with him in the horsebox to Aintree! She helped him settle down and went everywhere with him.

Poor Terry! He was not so lucky as Pat two years later when he and Gay

Gay Trip (centre) and Pat Taaffe clear Becher's in the 1970 National

Cheers! Rag Trade sticks his nose in as John Burke pours Fred Rimell a glass of champagne the day after their triumph in the 1976 National

Trip were beaten into second place by Well To Do. He did not get a good run going to Becher's second time; he had a horse on his inside that kept jumping right-handed and taking him out of his ground and he had to give a lot of ground away. But I always thought Terry should have won on him.

I like to see jockeys go down the middle in the National because if there is any trouble you can move one way or the other. But if you are stuck on the inside and three or four horses fall, they can take you into the wing and you've nowhere to go. Second time round it's different—you begin to move to the inside and go the shortest way from then on because they've thinned themselves out.

Rag Trade, the horse who completed my National four-timer in 1976, was completely different from the other three—he was the biggest, ugliest, most horrible-looking horse you have ever seen; a terrifically strong horse, like a tank, but a common horse.

His owner, hairdresser 'Teasy Weasy' Raymond, bought him for 18,000 guineas specifically, I think, to win his second National having won the race in 1963 with Ayala.

Rag Trade had previously been trained in the north by George Fairbairn before Teasy Weasy bought him and sent him to Arthur Pitt at Epsom and then on to Kinnersley. John Francome rode him into tenth place in the 1975 National—and said he'd never ride him again. He frightened the living soul out of John! But John Burke got on wonderfully well with him. Rag Trade would probably only get three or four inches off the ground at a fence but he could get away with hitting fences. He was tough and, of course, an out-and-out stayer who galloped for ever.

I remember one of the Stipendiary Stewards coming up to me after he won the Welsh Grand National at Chepstow in February 1976 and saying, 'Well, Fred, you won, but you'd have been a bit worried if you'd seen him jump the first in the straight. He never left the ground and broke the guard rail on the take-off side and broke it on the landing side, too!' He went right through the fence but it made no difference to him whatsoever.

Naturally enough, I had my reservations about the 1976 National but his owner was keen to run and he'd got round the previous year so he had to run again. I thought he was a dead stayer. He was such an in and out jumper, though by the time Aintree arrived, I felt he had improved and Burke got on with him wonderfully well. I think they just got used to each other—John actually made that horse.

He certainly gave him a glorious ride in the National. He said afterwards that they almost went at the fourth but after that they were always going well in the middle of the field. He was in third place as they came back on to the racecourse and Red Rum, who at that time was trying to win his third National, jumped the last with Eyecatcher. Rag Trade did not like to be in front too long and John organised him very well. He got after him at the elbow and the old horse just ran on and outstayed them with Red Rum two lengths back in second and Eyecatcher a further eight lengths behind.

That win put me in the record books: the first man to train four National winners. Saturday, 3 April 1976 was, indeed, a memorable day.

# MICHAEL STOUTE

Shergar's runaway victory in the 1981 Derby by a record ten lengths, was, naturally, a great thrill . . . just as Fair Salina's victory in the 1978 Oaks had been, for that was my first Classic success. But my Greatest Training Triumph? It may surprise many, but I have no doubt that it was overcoming several disappointments and setbacks before winning the 1973 Ayr Gold Cup with Blue Cashmere.

I have never experienced anything like it in my life. The build up before the race; I've never had a gut feeling like it before and I never will again, I'm sure I won't. I won't let myself. Let me explain . . .

In 1965 I took a job with Malton trainer Pat Rohan and later joined Doug Smith in Newmarket for two years before moving to Harry Thomson Jones. By the middle of 1971, I had decided to set up on my own. A week before the Yearling Sales started, I knew I could get the Cadland Stables for the following season though I would be unable to move in until the January of 1972.

When I set up, Raymond Clifford-Turner, a London solicitor to whom I'd been introduced by a mutual friend, was good enough to say I could spend £8,000 on a yearling. I was getting anxious, however, because I'd underbid on a couple; finally, on the Saturday morning of the Houghton Sales I bought one from the Cleaboy Stud for £9,000—that was Blue Cashmere.

He was a horse full of quality, a brown colt by Kashmir II out of Blessed Again by Ballymoss. He was a little bit long on his back but he was an important horse for me. He stood out among the twelve yearlings I had bought that year—none of the others had cost more than £2,800.

My wife, Pat, who had once been a race-reader for *Raceform*, and I were living in a flat in Newmarket at the time but Tom Jones and Jeremy Hindley were absolutely marvellous to me. Tom Jones had an overflow at Jeremy's Kremlin House Stables and he allowed me to put my yearlings there until

Cadland Stables became available. We used to break them in the afternoons with Tom Jones's staff and I must say that Fred Flippance, who is his head man now, was a great help. Blue Cashmere was very easy to handle and everything went smoothly with him.

The winter over, Pat and I were installed in Cadland Stables ready and raring to go. Then I suffered my first disappointment—Blue Cashmere was coming along nicely when he pulled a muscle so I had to be patient with him.

I couldn't run him until the first week of August—in the Duxford Maiden Stakes at Newmarket over six furlongs. I thought he would win; he was made third favourite but ran very green and was unplaced, though we couldn't condemn him on that. Frankie Durr, who rode him that day, had already taken to the horse after riding him in a lot of his work; he loved him and had a high opinion of him which I valued very much.

Just over six weeks later, I sent him to Yarmouth for the Hastings Maiden Plate; he was again third favourite at 100–30 but this time won by three lengths from the favourite Summer Knave with his head in his chest. Terrific! He was reasonably handicapped for his Nursery and I picked out a nice one worth £4,000 at Newmarket to finish off his two-year-old career. Then disappointment again; he bruised a foot so that was that until the following season.

We had moved to Beech Hurst on the Bury Road by then and from fifteen horses in my first year, I now had thirty; and high hopes for Blue Cashmere. Mr Clifford-Turner had been patient, never putting me under pressure, taking the disappointments of that first year magnificently.

And it looked as if everything was coming right when Blue Cashmere came out as a three-year-old and won the 6-furlong Queen Elizabeth Handicap at Kempton over Easter very impressively indeed. He had 7st 12 lbs and Paul Cook rode him; he settled well and came from the back of the field to lead in the final furlong and win by two lengths going away from Elizabeth Wales.

After that, I thought he would be an ideal horse for the 1-mile Britannia Stakes at Royal Ascot because he was by Kashmir II who had won the Guineas. Alas, another setback; soon after the Kempton race, he had a runny nose and coughed a bit—another, this time vital, hold-up in his work.

I did get him to Royal Ascot but he was only just right and finished ninth of twenty-two. He made headway two out but weakened in the final furlong. But I thought we'd try again over a mile—this time in the Welbred Handicap at Beverley two weeks later. It was the first time he had met really soft ground, the heavens opened up and then the fog came down and we could only see the last furlong of the race; and there he was, out the back door, he just couldn't go in the ground. It was a terrible disappointment.

There were more problems to come as he bruised a foot again soon after that race. He was a little bit thin-soled and always had problems with his feet so from then on we had him shod on pads and just removed them when he had his plates on for racing. I was learning about him all the time, of course; sometimes you never get the key to a horse but it's a challenge and Blue Cashmere was an important challenge.

I realised that not only did he want faster ground but he was getting a little freer at home all the time so he probably didn't stay. I decided to get him ready for the Northumberland Sprint Trophy Handicap for three-year-olds at Newcastle; I didn't have him spot on but I wanted him to have another race as it was now the middle of August. I just thought he'd run well and he went up to Newcastle more in hope than anything else.

What a marvellous surprise! Ernie Johnson rode him for the first time and he won by a length from Mayday Melody; for the first time in his life, things just slotted into place and everything went terribly smoothly. Now to take on the older horses! I decided then not to give him another race and risk a penalty for the Ayr Gold Cup—but there were five weeks to go before the Ayr race and they turned out to be the longest five weeks of my life.

Shortly before the Newcastle win, another of my three-year-olds, Alphadamus, squeezed home by a head from the Lester Piggott-ridden Home Guard in the Spillers Stewards Cup at Goodwood, so the Ayr race, as the last major 6-furlong handicap, became doubly significant for our stable. Apart from anything else, I wanted Blue Cashmere to justify himself; we knew he was a decent horse and Mr Clifford-Turner had been extremely understanding throughout. I desperately wanted him to win.

The waiting was agony. I've never felt such a build up to any race before or since—not even before Shergar's Derby.

It was a feeling of real expectation after all the horse had been through. I was worried about keeping him right, and had to take every possible precaution while he was on the walking grounds on the Heath in the final two weeks before the race in case he trod on a flint or something.

Mind you, strange as it may sound after all the problems, he was a gentleman of a horse, he was an easy horse to handle. Sometimes I'd work him on his own because he was a sprinter that would always do his work; he didn't need company, he'd often do solo work and I just gave him company if I felt he wanted a change. I got Ernie Johnson, who was to ride him at Ayr, to ride him in a gallop with Alphadamus. Blue Cashmere absolutely murdered him and that, of course, merely added to my excitement.

*Opposite page*
Blue Cashmere out on his own winning the Ayr Gold Cup

At last, the week of the race. I packed Blue Cashmere off in a box on his own—he was only my second runner ever at Ayr, incidentally—and he left with my head man, Jock Brown, on the Tuesday, three days before the race.

Michael Stoute greets Blue Cashmere after their triumph in the 1973 Ayr Gold Cup. 'I've never experienced anything like it in my life,' said Stoute

They broke their journey at Catterick for the horse to have a feed and a drink.

It was a big moment for Jock, too. He'd ridden the horse in most of his work and become attached to him as well which is why he, and not the travelling head lad, went to Ayr. Jock gave him a canter at Ayr on the Thursday and Friday mornings and I was to fly up first thing on the Friday, 21 September.

What a morning! It was pouring with rain at Newmarket. My mind began to race away with me; would it be raining in Ayr? We knew the horse wouldn't go on the soft; would my plane be able to take off? I couldn't stay at home and watch the race on television after all this. I was really in a state.

I was in a daze as I drove to catch the plane, and relieved to have the company of David Minton of the Curragh Bloodstock Agency to take my mind off things. As soon as I arrived on the racecourse, I checked with Jock and went to see Blue Cashmere; he was fine, no doubt wondering what all the fuss was about. All I wanted now was for the race to be over. I didn't know how to occupy myself; I didn't feel like much to eat, wasn't too interested in the other races. At last, the preliminaries over, I made my way to the stand where I joined Gavin Pritchard-Gordon and David Minton.

They're off! I picked up Mr Clifford-Turner's yellow and mauve colours easily enough and Blue Cashmere was never going to be beaten. After all that had gone before, I was managing to take the race calmly until Gavin and David started to shout at about the 2-furlong marker and then I let rip . . . I can tell you, he was shouted home all right! It was such a tremendous thrill. He was the first class horse I had ever trained and now he'd won a class race, taking on older horses and giving eighteen opponents a beating; in fact, he had three lengths to spare at the line from Parbleu.

I flew straight back and was home indoors within a few hours. I phoned Mr Clifford-Turner, who had had to stay in London and watch the race on television; he was overjoyed, too. Pat had asked some friends in and we sank a few bottles of champagne that night.

And Blue Cashmere? He went on to win the Trafalgar House Handicap at Ascot eight days later before stamping himself a champion the following year by winning the Nunthorpe at York and then the Temple Stakes at Sandown in 1975. After his racing career was over, he went to the Meddler Stud at Newmarket and I've trained a couple of his winners since.

# JEREMY TREE

My first Classic winner, Only For Life, was the highlight of a memorable week for me when he won the Two Thousand Guineas at Newmarket on Wednesday, 1 May 1963—apart from anything else, I had backed him at 66–1 and coupled him with Spree for the One Thousand! Even now, after almost thirty years of training at Beckhampton in Wiltshire, I think Only For Life's victory remains the Greatest Triumph of my career.

There have been many other marvellous moments. Though I have never trained a great quantity of winners, I have been very lucky and have had my share of relatively high-class horses although I don't think I've yet been fortunate enough to have a real crack. There have been other Classic victories with Juliette Marny (1975) and Scintillate (1979) each winning the Oaks while Known Fact won the 1980 Two Thousand Guineas; there have been stayers like Double Bore, Persian Road, John Cherry and Bright Finish; good middle-distance horses in Quiet Fling, Tiber, Midnight Marauder and Spree; sprinters such as D'Urberville, Swing Easy, Constans, Sharpo and Double Jump, possibly the most brilliant of them all, who sadly at the end of his two-year-old career broke a blood vessel rather badly in the Middle Park and had to be retired when this trouble re-occurred in training the following spring.

Only For Life, however, was very special to me. My uncle, Peter Beatty, who had won the 1938 Derby with Bois Roussel, died tragically in 1949 having gone blind. He left me his broodmares and foals, among which was a filly by Court Martial out of Borobella, a Bois Roussel mare. In 1951, I had the filly named Life Sentence in training at Newmarket with Dick Warden, with whom I was at that time pupil-cum-assistant.

Life Sentence was a pretty good two-year-old who ran eight times, twice finishing second and twice third as well as winning twice at Newmarket. I remember her finishing second in the Princess Mary Nursery at Doncaster when 'much expected', and ridden by a small claiming apprentice named Joe Mercer!

Because it appeared she was not really the type to train on and because I badly needed financial aid to keep some horses in training and to pay for the mares at Stud, Life Sentence was sold at the December Sales to Miss Gladys Yule, an action I subsequently greatly regretted. Borobella's next foal turned out to be Double Bore by Borealis a good stayer, and the first decent horse I trained. He won six races for me including the 1954 Newmarket St Leger and the Goodwood Cup, and the following year's Old Newton Cup. He really gave me a helping hand, probably a good deal more of one than I was able to give him.

Miss Yule sent Life Sentence to Michael Pope who did very well with her. Having just been beaten in the Princess Elizabeth Stakes at Epsom, Life Sentence went on to win a couple of races as a three-year-old in 1952, including the Red Rose Stakes at Manchester. At that time Miss Yule had a stallion, Flocon, who was not much of a success and poor Life Sentence was frequently sent to him, breeding some small winners, but I felt she would have made a good broodmare if given the chance to visit top stallions.

Then in the Newmarket yearlings sale catalogue of 1961, I saw a yearling colt by Chanteur—Life Sentence; I took an interest at once as Chanteur was a good stallion, who had been a tough, top class racehorse. His stock were apt to be plain and liked soft ground. I went to see the colt at Newmarket. Unfortunately he had been named already and horribly so in 'Dartmoor Ditty'.

What I saw certainly lived up to the plain side of the Chanteurs: he was a tall colt, all legs and arms with a big ugly head that didn't seem to fit his body; he also had two great big curbs on his hocks. However, there was something to like about him—he walked with great spring like his mother, so I bought him, without an order, for 1,600 guineas.

Miss Monica Sheriffe, who had already been an owner of mine, had started her successful career with a couple of good two-year-olds, half-brothers Prime Boy and Quentin, and had said she might buy another one. I offered her the Chanteur colt but only on condition she changed his name; she was reluctant to do this, like many people believing it would be unlucky. Eventually she agreed and named him 'Only For Life'; subsequently I rather wished she hadn't or anyway that I had kept a bit of him!

When we got back to Beckhampton, he immediately became so lame that we could not break him until we had his curbs pin-fired, after which they were never any more trouble. I remember little of his early days except him being big and gawky with a very nice disposition, and a big climbing action that hit the ground very hard.

When I started training at Beckhampton in 1953, I was lucky enough to have a wonderful head man, Bill Whelan, who had been head man to the great Frank Butters. To me, he was guide, Nannie, teacher and a great character. One evening, the late, and by me, much lamented, Jack Clayton came round stables. Jack had found Whelan for me and they were great friends, but I remember his look of blank amazement and disbelief when Whelan announced to him that this ugly big two-year-old, reminded him very much of the 1935 Derby winner, Bahram, at the same stage. I don't know who was the most surprised, Jack or me.

Only For Life took quite a time to come to hand and ran for the first time at Ascot on 27 September 1962; he started the 100–8 outsider of six, running for the Clarence House Stakes and carried 3 lbs overweight for the services of Jimmy Lindley, who was at that time my stable jockey. I seem to remember we expected him to run quite well, but were surprised when he made up ground in the last couple of furlongs to sweep through to a convincing win by three quarters of a length. Jack, who really didn't much approve of running horses at all and certainly not as two-year-olds, turned to Monica Sheriffe and said, 'Your trainer has obviously ruined what would have been quite a decent horse.'

Only For Life ran once more aged two, in the Houghton Stakes at Newmarket on 17 October when he had to give away a lot of weight, and where the ground was quite firm. He ran reasonably well but we learned that day what we were to discover several times the next season, that with his feet and high action, he simply could not act on any form of firm ground.

We had one of the coldest winters in memory from early January 1963 until the beginning of March; there was deep snow and hard frost, but bright sunshine during the days. When I returned from holiday in mid-February, the horses had been trotting round a paddock on a straw bed for six weeks. They looked exceptionally well and when the weather broke and they started cantering, it was plain they were surprisingly fit; the cold clear weather had suited them well and the effort of trotting in deep snow had made them fit.

Only For Life's first race as a three-year-old was to be the Greenham at Newbury on 20 April and as my horses had been running very well—Ros Rock, much inferior to Only For Life, had won the Free Handicap and Spree just been beaten half a length giving 10 lbs to Paddy Prendergast's good filly Gazpacho the day before in the Fred Darling—hopes for the Greenham were quite high. The ground was very heavy and there was a patch of false ground just under a furlong from home from which Newbury had trouble for some time, but which has now been drained.

My most vivid memory of the race was a furlong from home when Lavinia Duchess of Norfolk, who was standing next to me on top of the stand, patted me on the back and said, 'Well done, you have trotted up.' At almost the same moment, Only For Life went into this bog and stopped as if he had been shot; he finished third beaten a head and four lengths.

As I had warned Jimmy Lindley about this patch, I was not best pleased and my humour was not improved by his telling me the horse was cantering when he had blown up! However, Only For Life subsequently became 66–1 for the Two Thousand Guineas, and I availed myself of those odds with Heathorns as well as having a sporting double on Only For Life and Spree for the One Thousand which worked out at something like £75,000 to £100.

Only For Life did a really good gallop between Newbury and Newmarket with Ros Rock and a good four-year-old of Mr Jock Whitney's called Miletus and our hopes were very high. However, the weather changed and I remember leaving home for Newmarket on the Tuesday afternoon, on a cloudless day, thinking our chance had gone. That year, Guineas week started on Tuesday, with the Two Thousand on Wednesday and One Thousand on Thursday. I stayed with friends near Newmarket, and the fates were with us. It started to rain at 3.00 a.m. and never let up all morning; by the time the Guineas was run, it was soft, a rare occurrence at Newmarket.

Crocket, trained by Geoffrey Brooke, started a hot favourite at 5–2 and we were 33–1. I watched from the top of the stand which, in those days, one could easily reach; now, since the advent of escalators, the access has been made too easy, and I defy any owner or trainer with a runner in a big race at Newmarket who has to be in the paddock, to see a race except on television!

I remember little of the race though I clearly recall Only For Life reaching a prominent position as they came down the hill, and looking like a winner; then Ionian in Mrs Biddle's colours loomed up on the outside and went past him. The game seemed up, but Only For Life battled back and was gaining again in the last 100 yards. They flashed past the post seemingly locked together but as we were on the inside the angle had to favour me. I hurried down to the unsaddling enclosure to find Jimmy had ridden Only For Life into second place saying he thought he was just beaten; Liam Ward followed into the winner's enclosure, because he had nowhere else to go, but protesting he had not won either. I followed Jimmy into the weighing-room, where he turned to me as he sat on the scales, saying, 'We've won.' I returned outside, no decision . . . the loudspeaker system had chosen that moment to break down and, after what seemed an endless wait, someone looked at the board and the number, our number was in the frame first. We had actually won, by quite a short head, but enough!

I have always found the best part of winning any race, is waking up the next morning and realising that it really happened—and if it is a big race, that is likely to be very early, like around 4 o'clock! The morning after the Two Thousand was doubly sweet as I was pursued around Newmarket by Heathorns representatives trying to persuade me to lay off part of my double which luckily was each-way. I did lay off some, but in the event Spree ran the race of her life and was second, beaten only a length by the French-trained Hula Dancer who had started 2–1 on; a real run for my money and a never-to-be-forgotten week. Until I am lucky enough to train a Derby winner, it will have to do!

*Opposite page*
Only For Life (far side) and Ionian locked together at the finish of the 1963 Two Thousand Guineas

# FULKE WALWYN

Diamond Edge's victory in the 1981 Whitbread Gold Cup at Sandown, after nearly everyone else had written him off, probably gave me more satisfaction than any other winner—and I've been fortunate enough to train over 1,900. I still get a tremendous thrill every time I switch on the video and see him striding up the Sandown hill that day with the courage that has been his hallmark.

He had courage and brilliance that twice saw him made favourite for the Cheltenham Gold Cup—a race that only brought disappointment. We had to withdraw him on the morning of the 1979 Gold Cup because he had been cast in his box; a picture on my wall shows him beating Alverton, the winner of that race, just six weeks before the National Hunt Festival in the Leisure Caravan Parks Chase at Sandown. The following year, Diamond Edge gave 9 lbs and a four-length beating to Tied Cottage in the same Sandown race—then named the Freshfield Holidays Chase—and the Irish horse also went on to win the Gold Cup though he was subsequently disqualified.

Between those two Gold Cups, Diamond Edge had carried 11st 11 lbs to victory in the 1979 Whitbread and the form book confirms him to have been a worthy Cheltenham favourite though he was pulled up before the last in Tied Cottage's race. We had the virus that season, every horse in the yard was affected and Diamond Edge had it twice; as a result, he ran only four times, still managing to win three nice chases. He was a very sick horse when he got home and we had to give up any hopes of training him for the Whitbread.

I have had him since 1977 as a six-year-old; he is 16.3, a fine, strong honest horse, whose owner, Sam Loughbridge, is a vet in Exeter. He bought Six of Diamonds, the mare, in foal carrying Diamond Edge by Honour Bound for only about £250. The only subsequent progeny was a filly who never saw the racecourse.

The parents of one of my jockeys, Stuart Shilston, who was then an amateur, live at Exeter and knew Sam. They'd seen Diamond Edge run in point-to-points and suggested to Sam that he came to Lambourn. Amazingly enough, Diamond Edge had run five times in point-to-points and won only once which, in fact, was the only time he completed the course. He was a bit wild in those days and even ran out in one race.

We didn't have any great ideas about him in the early stages. We thought chasing was his job and Stuart rode him in his first race, the Festive Novices Chase at Chepstow on 12 November 1977, because he had introduced the horse to us. But Diamond Edge made a bad mistake at the first in the straight last time round and unshipped Stuart; it wasn't his fault but Sam and I agreed the horse was a bit too much for Stuart and Bill Smith has subsequently ridden him in all his races. Stuart has since made his name as a good horseman and a very competent jockey.

Diamond Edge always takes a very strong hold but he has a great temperament. He's keen, really even now a bit too keen, but he's a wonderful doer and a grand game horse to train. He has always had the same lad looking after him, Mick Whelehan, affectionately nicknamed Mullingar, who is undoubtedly very fond of Diamond Edge—as is Jack Maguire, head man in the lower yard. Diamond Edge has had his troubles with the bloody virus, not leg trouble, but on his day, as he's shown, when things go right he's a very good horse.

Things didn't turn out right though when he began his 1980–81 campaign on 17 October in the Pretentious Chase over 2½-miles at Lingfield. He would have trotted up but jumped the second last a bit crooked and gave Bill no chance of staying on; but Bill said he was still running away and was really pleased with him for, apart from that one error, he jumped well.

Shortly afterwards he went to Wincanton and won the Terry Biddlecombe Chase very easily. He then won the McEwans Lager Chase at Cheltenham on 5 December fairly comfortably, beating Highway Patt which had been brought over from Ireland by Mick O'Toole and then sold to David Nicholson. He gave him 27 lbs and beat him half a length—this was his warm-up race for the King George. The horse seemed in good form at home on the downs and was very well in himself and we felt hopeful, but no more than that because Kempton's not really his track, it's too sharp for him. Kempton was the only place he had ever fallen—it's too fast and too flat for him; he likes a good galloping course with plenty of work to do. Anaglogs Daughter went off at a million miles an hour in the King George and made it even worse for Diamond Edge because Bill always sets him off a little bit steady so he can hold him better in the early stages. However, he finished third and was running on strongly at the finish.

Diamond Edge
follows Father
Delaney over the final
fence in the 1981
Whitbread Gold Cup
at Sandown

Diamond Edge came back from Kempton all right. After talking to Bill about it afterwards, I realised he had been flat out all the way. He's always such a keen horse at home, even if he's not at his best, he's a natural puller and stupidly one didn't spot it. We ran him next in the Mildmay at Sandown over 3 miles 5 furlongs. He had top weight of 12st but he didn't please us really, finishing fourth. I thought he was going to win at the Pond fence but he made a shocking jump at the second last and again at the last. He might have won if he'd really jumped those last two fences. He was very much in contention upsides. We were disappointed.

We went to Sandown again on 7 February to bid for a hat-trick in the 3-mile Freshfields Chase. He had 11st 11 lbs while Night Nurse carried top weight of 12st. But again it wasn't a very satisfactory race—Diamond Edge made more mistakes than usual and finished fifth. We began to think there was something wrong. We couldn't think why he was making all these mistakes. Bill said he switched off the ignition at the last fence. We started worrying.

His owner brought in a specialist from Exeter, largely because Sam thought he was making a noise; I was convinced he wasn't. Until then, we'd run him in a puckle nose band which did help Bill steady him and kept his head in the right place. We made various experiments at Saxon House with and without the nose band and exhaustive tests—but couldn't find anything wrong with him.

One Sunday morning, with an electric device round his neck, we cantered him round first of all in the loose school while the experts listened in with earphones. I didn't think he was making a noise, but they did. Then they wanted to try him on grass but he got a bit gee'd up and had to go up the gallop about six times. By the end he was really whipping round. He always goes out in big rubber-lined leather boots because he whips round like nobody's business and he could hit himself doing this. Thank heavens for those boots; even so, that night I thought he had a tendon. There was heat and soreness. I thought, 'Christ, this is it.' I rang and told the owner that he would need a few very quiet days; we would just hope for the best and let it go down naturally. There was nothing else we could do. And this was two weeks before Cheltenham. Thank God, it was only a blow because it did look and feel like a tendon. The swelling went down all right but it delayed him a bit—luckily he was a very fit horse.

We managed to run him in the Gold Cup, and did so without the puckle nose band. Neither Bill nor I were very happy though he seemed all right at home without it. Nor was I happy about the state of the ground which was desperately heavy, but he ran a much better race than his two previous outings and finished fifth, running on at the end which he hadn't been doing.

One thing that had come out of the many tests and experiments was that he was taking in too much dust. The specialist recommended that all his hay should be soaked in water for twelve hours before he ate it. We never thought he would eat it but he seemed to love it and has done so ever since. We have always damped our hay but had never heard of soaking it like this.

We really thought the Gold Cup would be his last race of the 1980–81 season and we did virtually nothing with him for the next couple of weeks. As usual he ate up well and was very full of himself. Sam agreed that he

Fulke Walwyn
receives his sixth
Whitbread Gold Cup
from the Queen
Mother after the
victory of Diamond
Edge

should be given one more chance in the Whitbread before having his annual holiday. I knew the Whitbread trip of virtually 3¾ miles and the Sandown track suited him well. I gave him his final preparation about ten days before the race and remember coming back into the house afterwards and telling my wife, Cath, how delighted I was with the way he had worked. Bill Smith was equally delighted and reminded me again that in his view the horse was always better when fresh, so that the very little work we had done with him since Cheltenham would be all to his advantage.

Perhaps as important as anything, the ground had dried up a good deal by the end of April and was just about perfect at Sandown. Naturally we were concerned about giving lumps of weight to the whole field—nevertheless it was with some confidence that he went to post as 5–1 favourite.

They set off at a cracking pace with first Betton Gorse and then Bobjob cutting out the pace. This time, we decided that Bill should lay up with the leaders from the time the field settled down. This worked out very well; he was in the first four from the start of the second circuit. He was not foot perfect along the railway fences but made no really serious mistake. Diamond Edge was still going easily as the field came to the Pond fence and at that moment I was quietly confident. But my enthusiasm soon faded as both John Francome on the lightly-weighted Ottery News and Alan Brown on Father Delaney went past us approaching the last. All three jumped it perfectly but Bill Smith, with perfect balance, drove our fellow up between the other two; he had a length and a half to spare from Father Delaney at the winning post with Ottery News a further three lengths back. What courage the horse had shown with his huge weight of 11st 7 lb and what a fantastic ride Bill had given him.

This was the twenty-fifth running of the Whitbread Gold Cup and my sixth victory in the race. I must say that as I walked to the winner's enclosure to receive the Cup from the Queen Mother, I felt somewhat vindicated in my continued belief in Diamond Edge, only the second horse to win this great race for the second time—Larbawn won it in 1968 and 1969. We went off to celebrate later that evening and it was somewhat ironic that I was telling everybody what a big factor the good ground had been, only to come out of the pub to find that snow was falling heavily and we were damn lucky to get home, where we remained snowed in for the next four days.

With my confidence restored, plenty of time to reflect and the huge advantage of hindsight, I reckoned that I had certainly learned something about this bold chaser in whom I had expressed so much faith. First of all, there was little doubt that Bill Smith was right about his being at his best when fresh. The way the King George had been run on Boxing Day took more out of the horse than I had realised and may well have accounted for his rather poor showing in the next two races at Sandown. Our early view that the horse was best suited by soft or even heavy ground was almost certainly proved wrong and had been based more on a judgement of his action than in racing. Possibly the veterinary experiments that had been carried out during the preparatory period for Cheltenham had slightly held him up in his work so he may not have been quite cherry ripe.

Diamond Edge had magnificently vindicated my confidence in him and, with that experience in mind, we did not run him again until the Hennessy Cognac Gold Cup's twenty-fifth anniversary race on 28 November. He was the only one of the fourteen runners not to have had a run in the new season, and he carried top weight of 11st 10 lbs to victory—my seventh in the race, and his thirteenth win from twenty-two races, taking his winnings to over £96,000. For me, a glittering diamond of a horse.

# PETER WALWYN

When I started training in 1960 after seven years learning about it all, I only then realised how little I knew about it—i.e. making the decisions etc. and that, until the day I die, will be an ongoing situation!

Twice in three years, I saw our hopes of a Derby winner dashed in the final furlong when first Shoemaker in 1969 and then Linden Tree in 1971 were caught, passed and beaten into second place behind Blakeney and Mill Reef. It seemed then that after two seconds, it would be a long time before another horse as good would come along. However, in no way were we disappointed—in fact, the reverse; we were thrilled at the way unconsidered outsiders had run so well. But at the end of the 1973 Flat season, Grundy came into our lives—the horse who was to realise our greatest ambition at Epsom on Wednesday, 4 June 1975, a day we'll never forget.

It was just fifteen years after we had started training, never thinking then that we would have a Derby winner. In 1960, I'd married a marvellous girl, Virginia, the sister of Nick Gaselee, and we decided to start training. With a legacy from my parents, we were able to buy Windsor House at Lambourn with thirty boxes and eleven acres, two cottages and a reasonable house for £12,000, which in these days seems unbelievable. We took every horse we could get within reason and gradually filled up the boxes and got going.

By 1964, we realised we were getting a bit short of room and it obviously wasn't going to be the ideal place for training top-class Flat race horses. Luckily, we were able to buy Seven Barrows just outside Lambourn from Mr and Mrs Derrick Candy with its 300 acres and marvellous gallops; we were on our way. The better class horses started to arrive and Mabel—who, to be fair, had been trained at Windsor House the season before—was second in the 1965 Oaks and won the Yorkshire Oaks, and we had those Derby seconds with Shoemaker and Linden Tree.

Then, in October 1973, bloodstock agent Keith Freeman paid 11,000 guineas at Tattersalls Sales at Newmarket on behalf of Dr Carlo Vittadini for a chestnut colt bred at the Overbury Stud by Great Nephew out of Word From Lundy; that was a very old and tough family of the Holland-Martins. It was a family I knew well because, when I was holding a licence for my cousin Helen Johnson Houghton at Blewbury in the late fifties, we had Miss McTaffy and Honey Parrot and others from the same family.

We had been training for Dr Vittadini since 1970 and took the colt, Grundy, to Seven Barrows. He was a glorious mover but considered by some to be a bit flash; he wasn't over big, but a real athlete. He was extremely hard to break in because he was so fiery and such a handful; he took much longer than most, but we persevered and got him going very quietly. Eventually he was ridden away loose and we got him cantering, but he was always boisterous; he would never harm anybody but he was always bouncing.

We started Grundy working in the spring of 1974. He moved well but was inclined to do too much, to try and tear the ground up, so we got him settled in behind other two-year-olds and he appeared to be much more restrained. But if he was shown daylight, he was inclined to go too free. We went to the Newmarket July meeting and Keith Freeman came up and asked me how the Great Nephew colt was. I said he was a lovely mover and although he was only starting working, looked a racehorse and I visualised him running at Ascot that month.

Having had further talks with Carlo Vittadini and Keith Freeman, we decided to run Grundy in the Granville Stakes over 6 furlongs at Ascot on 26 July for Grundy's racing debut; a race for colts and geldings that had not run. I ran another horse, No Alimony; my stable jockey, Pat Eddery, chose to ride Grundy with Willie Carson on No Alimony. In fact, No Alimony hit the front and it was only when a gap appeared that Grundy went by and won convincingly by two lengths from No Alimony. We wanted to give Grundy another race in reasonable company but he had a slightly dirty nose for a few days. However, he was soon fine again and we went to Kempton on 30 August for the 6-furlong Sirenia Plate; he led three and a half furlongs out and won impressively by two and a half lengths.

We then ran him in the Champagne Stakes over 7 furlongs at Doncaster on 11 September. It was his first Pattern race, a Group 2 and, from being tucked in with nowhere to go, a gap suddenly appeared a furlong out and he ran on well to win splendidly. He finished his two-year-old season by winning the William Hill Dewhurst Stakes over 7 furlongs at Newmarket on 18 October; the weather was miserable and the going very soft but Grundy pulled his way to the front two furlongs out and won by an extremely easy six lengths from Steel Heart, who had won the Gimcrack and Middle Park. After this, we thought we had a potential Classic horse on

Peter Walwyn . . .
'Grundy achieved our
greatest ambition.'

our hands but felt that although he'd been entered in the Derby, the Two Thousand Guineas would be his first target.

Grundy's form was franked by the fact that No Alimony was a close up third in the Observer Gold Cup at Doncaster to the French-trained Green Dancer, who was to be the eventual favourite for the 1975 Derby. The day after the Observer race, a Sunday racing correspondent wrote that he would be very surprised if No Alimony could not beat Grundy at distances of a mile or more; that if Grundy did, he would have to go to work! Thereupon, on the Sunday afternoon, I sent him a telegram which I later discovered had to be bicycled out several miles by a poor telegraph boy from Haywards Heath in Sussex, the Post Office worker obviously not knowing what was in the telegram. The telegram read: GO TO WORK [SIGNED] GRUNDY. The Sunday newspaper correspondent still laughs at the memory!

Grundy wintered well. I came back from my holiday in the Far East and the horse seemed in terrific form; but St Patrick's Day, 17 March, brought us only bad luck. Grundy walked into the covered ride and, just before the entrance to the track, he suddenly gave a leap forward and Corby, the horse in front, lashed out and kicked him straight on the front of the face. When I walked out to the yard, Grundy was coming back in with a dent in his face and blood pouring from his nostrils and mouth. I immediately rang our vet, Charles Frank, who lived nearby in Childrey.

They were anxious moments but Charles said there was nothing physically he could do bar put the horse on antibiotics. The honeycombed bone at the front of his face was kicked in but it was not near anything vital bar the sinuses and the worry was whether these would be affected. We had to wait for the antibiotics to do their work and, remarkably, within a fortnight or so the face was clearing up and Grundy was able to resume cantering. I don't think the injury actually bothered him too much; he just had to get over the physical effects which were a lot of clotting, bleeding and mucous coming from the nose for a few days. It was a miracle really but he was one of those horses that was really tough and able to cope—many would not have done so.

Anyhow, the horse recovered and we decided he needed a race before the Two Thousand Guineas; I chose the Clerical Medical Greenham Stakes at Newbury on Saturday, 19 April. It poured with rain a couple of days before and I called in to Newbury on the Thursday on my way back from the Newmarket Craven meeting and walked the course. There was a new strip of ground up the rail that had not been used the year before which I thought would probably be okay and wouldn't be bad ground, and they were going to race up the stands side. But in the meantime it poured again on the Friday night. Dr Vittadini came over from Milan and arrived at Seven Barrows in the morning; I decided to leave it to him whether to run the horse or not.

The horse desperately needed a race and this was the obvious one for him as the kick on the face had held up everything else. Dr Vittadini decided that the horse should run. 'The race will bring him on a lot,' I said, 'but do you mind if he gets beaten?' Dr Vittadini said, 'No, I don't, but we mustn't give the horse too hard a race in the circumstances.'

Grundy went to post odds-on in a field of nine—and suffered his first defeat, but he ran well and looked like winning before a horse of Clive Brittain's, Mark Anthony, came along and beat him by two lengths. However, I felt there was no reason why Mark Anthony should beat him again knowing what had happened.

That was quickly proved correct in the Two Thousand Guineas when Mark Anthony finished sixth—but Grundy again found one too good as this time Henry Cecil's Bolkonski beat him. It was, however, a very ragged race, delayed because of the action of some Newmarket striking stable lads who stood in front of the stalls to start with; in fact, the horses were taken round in front of the stalls and the race started by flag. Grundy hit the front at The Bushes but was run out of it by Bolkonski and beaten half a length running on again at the finish. He didn't have too hard a race and I felt he was improving all the time; he was really flourishing and coming to himself.

I felt his best chance of a Group 1 race for the time being would be the Irish Two Thousand Guineas—and Dr Vittadini agreed. So we went to The Curragh on 17 May and Grundy won very comfortably by one and a half lengths from Monsanto with Mark Anthony behind again, in third place. I drove down to the start on the morning of the race and when you stand there and look up, you see that it's a much stiffer mile than Newmarket with a very, very stiff finish. Grundy won in such style that Pat Eddery and I felt certain then that we should run him in the Derby which was just eighteen days away.

Yet up until then, I was still thinking in terms of Grundy being a miler; we'd got all the options open but it swung the other way after the Irish race. It's very difficult to plan a season's programme for a horse because they may not stay as far or may stay further than you think; therefore, you're much better off to play it by ear and go stage by stage with all your options open. One's got to be flexible because you're learning about a horse the whole time; the problem is they can't talk.

I was certain now that Grundy would get the 1½ miles of the Derby. From then on, really, all was plain sailing. The horse returned from Ireland; he ate everything, he didn't need an awful lot of work for he had already had three races, but we took him up to Moss Hill a week before Epsom, an ideal trial ground for the Derby. It has left-handed turns and a slant to the left as well, everything you like for an exercise gallop over the Derby distance.

Pat Eddery rode Grundy, Frank Morby was on Corby with Brian Taylor on Red Regent and Joe Mercer on No Alimony; they didn't overdo it and went one mile and a quarter. Grundy worked extremely well, he did it so smoothly that we were very happy and we had extra hopes that he'd run well at Epsom.

We always send our Derby horses to Epsom the day before the race; we do a canter round the paddock in the morning and then they go off. It's better for them both from a security angle and from a relaxing point of view with all the traffic and so on; they get there and they can relax. Epsom trainer Boggy Whelan very kindly lets us go down and use his private ground on the morning of the race out of the way of everybody. I saw Grundy off to the course at lunchtime.

My wife and I stayed in London as usual the night before and Grundy seemed fine and relaxed as I had hoped when I arrived the following morning. I had two other runners in the Derby—No Alimony, who had beaten the subsequent St Leger winner Bruni, and Red Regent, who had won two handicaps in very easy style; we were doubtful whether he would get the trip but thought he was entitled to have a run.

Nick Gaselee and Mark Smyly helped me saddle up the horses, then I went into the paddock for a final word with Pat Eddery before climbing the stairs to Lord Derby's box from where I had watched our filly Polygamy win the previous year's Oaks.

Eighteen horses went to post with Grundy second favourite at 5–1 behind Green Dancer. Red Regent led for the first couple of furlongs and then Anne's Pretender went on; Grundy was always travelling smoothly. He was fourth into Tattenham Corner but the result wasn't in doubt from about two furlongs out; he got up to Anne's Pretender in front, quickened up past Anne's Pretender and won nicely. I gave one roar and then I was down the steps to meet the horse; there was such a hubbub of excitement that I don't remember much after that. I know I was asked about the horse's plans and I said, 'I don't know about his plans but I know mine—I'm off to have a large drink!'

We were invited to the Queen's box and she congratulated the Vittadinis,

Grundy storms to victory in the 1975 Derby

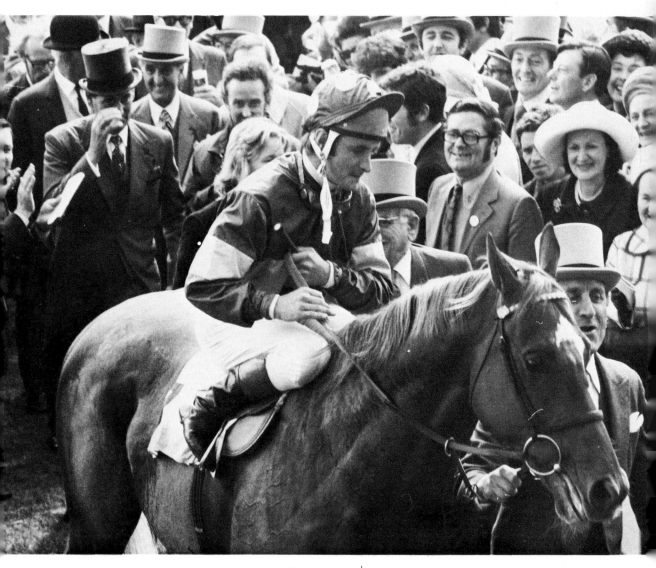

Owner Dr Carlo Vittadini leads in Grundy and Pat Eddery after their Derby triumph

Pat Eddery and myself; she was very kind and very interested to hear all about the horse as we chatted away. It was a marvellous day, and marvellous to win a Derby, too, with an English-bred horse.

I had a runner, Taros, in the Diomed Stakes a couple of races later and he should have won, too, but finished fourth in the end and after that we drove home to Lambourn. What a welcome we had at Seven Barrows; there were flags everywhere and someone had put up a great banner over the entrance. There must have been a hundred people in my house, drinking my drink—it was overwhelming. We waited for the horse to come home and seemed to play the video endlessly all evening, and finally I sank into bed at about 3 a.m.

The sweetest moment of all, perhaps, was when I fetched the papers from the back door at seven o'clock the next morning; just to read the paper that actually told us we had won the Derby, that was very nice. Then I rode out at 7.30 with the first string as always and as I rode alongside and watched the two-year-olds, I couldn't help thinking to myself, 'I wonder if there's a horse among these that might run well in the Derby next year.' That's what we're looking for, really.

We had that marvellous feeling of achievement; there were so many people who helped make the horse and got him to his peak on the day . . . Matt McCormack, who rode him virtually every day and certainly got him very settled; Ray Laing, my head lad; Charlie Johnson, the boy who looked after him; and last but not least Pat Eddery. But everyone at Seven Barrows shared in Grundy's triumph; these are all team things and it's rather unfair that one man should get the kudos. With a stable, there are so many people involved. It was a marvellous day. I may win another Derby, who knows, but the first is the one I'll never forget.

# DERMOT WELD

I knew Blue Wind was something special the way she beat a very good filly of mine, Overplay, by two and a half lengths at Leopardstown on 20 September 1980 in the 1-mile Silken Glider Stakes, the best two-year-old fillies race in Ireland with a view to Classic potential. I had no hesitation, therefore, in recommending Mr Bertram Firestone to pay 180,000 Irish pounds when Blue Wind came up at the Goffs November Sales.

My one ambition was to train a Classic winner. I'd been placed in all the Irish Classics that year; I'd twice trained over 100 winners in a season; I'd five times been leading Irish trainer in number of winners; and I'd won races like the Middle Park, Gimcrack, Queen Mary Stakes, Jersey Stakes, Stewards Cup, Cheveley Park Stakes, Coronation Stakes and Ribblesdale Stakes since first taking out a licence in 1972—but a Classic win had eluded me.

Blue Wind was the filly to change all that; a good-looking chestnut, 16.2, with a marvellous constitution and well bred. I'd already been successful with the offspring of her sire, Lord Gayle, who I considered very much underrated. I trained the top handicap horse in Ireland, Croghan Hill, and a very good filly named Gayshuka, both by Lord Gayle, who was himself a beautifully bred horse by Sir Gaylord out of Sticky Case by Court Martial; I saw no reason why he couldn't produce a Classic winner. There was a host of winners, too, on the dam's side, one of the best and oldest Irish families. Blue Wind's dam, Azuline, was third in the Irish One Thousand Guineas and fourth in the Irish Oaks and the first three dams were all Stakes winners.

The winter of 1980–81 was therefore one of eager anticipation and quiet optimism. Blue Wind progressed well and began to grow into her frame; she just did light exercise trotting round my indoor school during November and December and we gave her front fetlock joints a light working blister to tighten them up. We let her relax and put on weight and settle into her new environment. I do nothing strenuous at all with my horses during Novem-

Dermot Weld . . .
'Blue Wind was some
filly.'

ber and December and Day One to me is January One and that's when we started off Blue Wind properly. She did five or six miles trotting on the roads twice a week and some long, steady canters during January and February when the weather was quite mild. We had no hold-ups with her, she was a very sound, easy filly to train.

The only thing that concerned me was her coat; she was a filly that really thrived on the summer weather and sunshine and was backward in her coat. We had a lot of rain in March and the ground was pretty soft so her training was slightly curtailed for the one and only time. I had to scrap my plans to work her over six or seven furlongs in March and she just went at half-pace at the very most and even then only on the all-weather gallop. I also decided to skip the Athasi Stakes at The Curragh which I'd pencilled in as her prep race for the Irish One Thousand Guineas; instead, we waited until 2 May for Blue Wind's 1981 debut in the Edenderry Stakes at Phoenix Park, a 1-mile race open to colts and fillies. Wally Swinburn, my stable jockey, took his time on her, switched her to the outside with two furlongs to go and she went away to win by an easy length and a half.

My target was to have her at her peak for the Oaks at Epsom on 6 June and she still didn't have her summer coat when she ran in the Goffs Irish

One Thousand Guineas at The Curragh on 23 May; we'd had the wettest May on record and the going was officially soft, but nearer heavy and, in the circumstances, she ran an excellent, game race being beaten a short head by Arctique Royale, who herself on the day was a very good filly. I've no doubt that Blue Wind would have won easily if the ground had been good or even approaching good to soft; even so, she still would have won but for changing her stride and losing momentum about 100 yards out.

Epsom and her first attempt at 1½ miles was just thirteen days away and she'd had a much harder race than I would have liked; she was a fit filly all right, but I had to keep her mentally tuned and then just freshen her up. We gave her a couple of days off and then started back into light work. I decided on just one piece of fast work on the trial ground on the Flat Rath at The Curragh on the Wednesday before Epsom when she went a brisk seven furlongs with her lead filly, Citissima; she did it well and I was satisfied she would be at her peak for the most important race of her life. That was the last time she had a saddle on her back until Lester Piggot's saddle went on for the Oaks.

While Wally had ridden her very well in the Irish Guineas, Mr Firestone, his racing manager John Muldoon and myself, decided to book Lester for Epsom quite simply because he did not have a ride in the race and his skill and record at Epsom spoke for itself. There was nothing more to it than that.

Blue Wind flew to Epsom on the Thursday morning with two lads, Robert Scarf and Paddy Costello, while I stayed home. I knew she was a sensible filly and she was in good hands. They walked her round on the Thursday afternoon and Friday morning and I was delighted when I arrived at the racecourse stables early on Saturday morning to see she'd eaten up every crumb and looked superb; she'd obviously travelled well and had a skin on her like a seal.

I guess there was a spring in my step as I walked the course that morning. I was delighted to see how the track had dried out and that the going by then was good. I felt it would be an ideal ground for Blue Wind, the best on which she had ever run. I was quite happy that she'd handle the track, too; I didn't feel the downhill gradient or the bend would cause problems because, although she was a big, long-striding filly, she was pretty adaptable. I was quietly confident that with average luck she would win, and win well, and I would have trained that elusive Classic winner with my first runner in the Oaks which, in my opinion, is the finest race in the world for three-year-old fillies.

Then a funny thing happened on my way back to London that morning for breakfast with a friend and owner of mine, Michael Holleran. As I

*Opposite page*
Lester Piggott and Blue Wind storm home seven lengths clear of Madam Gay to win the 1981 Oaks

turned a corner, I came face to face with the Epsom trainer, Dermot 'Boggy' Whelan; indeed, I almost knocked him down as he led his string along. I thought that was too big a coincidence to ignore, for six years earlier Boggy had saddled Lanecourt for me when I became the first man to train and ride the winner of Epsom's Möet and Chandon Trophy, the Amateurs' Derby. Boggy had a great hello for me and I asked if he'd like to help me saddle Blue Wind that afternoon if he wasn't doing anything. He said he'd be delighted; I'm not really superstitious, but . . .

Boggy helped me saddle the filly and I left it to Lester to ride his own race for he'd spoken with Wally Swinburn about Blue Wind. She took quite a hold of Lester going down to the start, she was pretty keen and very well tuned for her race so I was pleased when they went a good gallop at the start, allowing Lester to drop her in and let her relax. After half a furlong, he had her lobbing along perfectly. I was happy all the way and my only concern came when they rounded Tattenham Corner with Leap Lively about four lengths clear, followed by three fillies with Blue Wind a couple of lengths behind them. For a moment, I found myself wondering whether we would catch Leap Lively; would Leap Lively get too far away?

I soon had the answer; the very second Lester switched Blue Wind to the outside and put her into overdrive, it was all over. Even before she got near Leap Lively or Madam Gay, I knew we'd win it. It was only a question of how far she'd win by because I had full confidence in her stamina and knew, with her speed, she could pick up ground and fly. She flew all right, storming home by seven lengths from Madam Gay with Leap Lively another ten lengths further back in third. Blue Wind's time of 2 minutes 40.93 seconds was almost four seconds faster than Shergar's 2 minutes 44.21 for the Derby the previous Wednesday. It may have been Lester's twenty-fifth English Classic, it was my first, and there's never been a victory like it.

We flew back to Dublin that evening for a celebration in Jockey Hall at The Curragh. Six weeks later and Blue Wind became the first Irish-trained filly to complete the English-Irish Oaks double, winning The Curragh Classic by two and a half lengths from Condessa; Blue Wind was some filly and she'll always be something special to me.

*Opposite page*
The smile on the face of Lester Piggott says it all as he and Blue Wind are led in after winning the Oaks

# FRED WINTER

My greatest training triumph was turning a bumptious, confident, over-cocky young American into a courageous and winning rider of the Grand National in only his fifth race over English fences. I am amazed even now when I look back and recall the single-mindedness with which the twenty-seven-year-old amateur, Tommy Smith, came, saw and conquered Aintree, the toughest jump course in the world, on Saturday, 27 March 1965.

Yet for me, it all began by chance three years earlier when I flew to the States to ride what turned out to be a non-runner in a steeplechase. I was fortunate enough to be offered a spare ride in another race—and won; afterwards, I chatted awhile with Phyllis Mills, the sister of Mimi van Cutsem, mentioning that I would be setting up as a trainer in the next year or two.

I thought nothing more of it until the early summer of 1964 when I received a transatlantic call from a Mr Tommy Smith, a friend of Phyllis Mills. He had recently won the Maryland Hunt Cup for the second successive year on a horse called Jay Trump and wanted to send him to Britain for a crack at the National.

Tommy told me he was contemplating sending the horse to Dan Moore in Ireland and asked my opinion but, in passing, mentioned that the horse disliked soft ground. That gave me the encouragement I needed. 'Send him to England,' I told Tommy. 'In Ireland, the purses are smaller and the going deeper. The horse's best chance of qualifying for the National is here. I suggest you send the horse to me. I've just started training and only have a few horses. He'll get more personal attention than he would in a larger yard.'

He didn't need any more persuading, and the first chapter of what I consider one of racing's most amazing stories had been completed.

Tommy married Frances Cochran, a member of one of Maryland's oldest and most influential families in the June of 1964 but even his wedding plans took a back seat as he set out on the road to Aintree. I have never seen such obsessive determination, such a will to win.

For my part, I didn't really know what to expect. I discovered that Jay Trump, a bay, had been bred by a man called Jay Sensenich. The horse's dam, Be Trump, was a fifty-dollar purchase and an utter failure as a racehorse; his sire, Tonga Prince, was a moderate performer at the tiny Charles Town track in West Virginia. Jay Trump was bred to be nothing— and very nearly was.

Tommy Smith went to the stables at Charles Town looking for a horse for Mrs Mary Stephenson who farmed in Ohio; she was a childhood friend of Tommy's mother in Cincinnati. Tommy was attracted to a three-year-old with an excellent temperament but, as they say in the States, 'a touch of the slows'. But on his last Charles Town start on 23 June 1960, Jay Trump ran like crazy and was beaten three-quarters of a length at 84–1. The asking price on Jay Trump had been 1,250 dollars; after that run, Tommy had to go to 2,000 dollars to secure him for Mrs Stephenson. So the horse went to Warburton Farm in Maryland's Western Run valley in the heart of the Green Spring Hounds hunting country where trainer Bobby Fenwick moulded the future champion. By the time Fenwick was finished, Jay Trump was Tommy Smith's dream horse—the horse to win a National— and from the moment they won their second Maryland Hunt Cup on 25 April 1964, he lived only for his dream.

The gelding had been booked to fly Pan Am and the airline built a special stall in their new 707 making its maiden transatlantic run; Jay Trump was insured for 60,000 dollars. Tommy returned from his honeymoon in mid-July to collect Jay Trump and hit his first snag; the stall Pan Am had constructed was two and a half feet too small.

Tommy was left at Kennedy International Airport holding his horse and a bag of the best Canadian Double Recleaned Alberta Oats while the plane flew to England without them. Eventually, BOAC were persuaded to build a special stall and after two agonising days sharing the RSPCA shelter at Kennedy with a contingent of monkeys, Tommy and Jay Trump headed across the Atlantic, arriving at Heathrow on 16 July where Frances, his bride of a few weeks, and the Lambourn Racehorse Transport Service horse-box awaited them. They arrived at Uplands yard at midnight.

Jay Trump was none the worse for the journey but did not look his best. He had been let down following his last race the previous April. He had a grass belly and his coat had lost its shine.

We didn't get off to a very good start the first morning when Tommy walked into the yard to ride out. 'It's now ten to eight. We always start at a quarter to,' I told him. He was never late again. I decided to put Tommy up

on Anglo, the horse who was to win the 1966 National for me. No sooner was he up than he was off again, unceremoniously dumped on the ground. I could see the other lads having a grin and it wasn't difficult to read their thoughts. There was a lot of work to do if Mr T. Smith was going to achieve his life's ambition.

The longer I knew Tommy the more I realised just how totally consumed his whole life had been with winning the National. He was the third generation of amateur steeplechase riders whose grandfather Harry Worcester Smith and father Crompton never tired of discussing Aintree and the Grand National. Neither had been able to ride in the race; Tommy vowed that he would—and that he would win. An illustrated map of the Grand National course hung over the fireplace at Featherbed Farm, a house in the heart of the Virginia fox-hunting country where Tommy was christened Crompton Jr; in order to distinguish him from his father, his mother nicknamed him Tommy.

Frances and Tommy settled into Lambourn; they stayed at first in the bridal suite at the Red Lion Hotel but in the September of 1964 moved to Kapal Cottage at the end of Upper Lambourn village, leasing it from the Harbour Master of Singapore. Tommy cycled to Uplands every day, riding out Jay Trump with the first lot and choosing to 'do' his horse himself; that helped him indoctrinate himself with our way of life. Then he cycled home for breakfast before returning to ride out again with the second lot.

Tommy's attention to detail was staggering. Before the horse had been flown to England, he worked out every possible item so that Jay Trump arrived without missing an oat. He set out to discover the equivalent nutritional value of British foodstuffs and the necessary substitutes which would equalise Jay Trump's American diet. Tommy's younger sister Kitty undertook a 'comparative study of the nutrition of the horse in training in the United States and in England'; Kitty's fifteen-page paper contained the most detailed analysis of the foodstuffs in the respective countries and exhaustive studies showing 'the total digestive nutrients offered to animals.'

Tommy himself was clearly such a good rider that we hardly had to change his style or ways at all. He did, like many Americans, ride on his toes rather than on the ball of the foot, but as he had been so successful riding that way, I felt he was best left alone even though I myself don't particularly like it. My main objective was to teach him race-riding in England; that's a very different thing from race-riding in the States.

The closing date for entries for the National was 6 January and before we could even enter Jay Trump, we had to qualify him. I had tried to bring Jay Trump along slowly and carefully, refusing to take chances on what I considered the too-firm ground. Everyone in the yard had taken to the horse

*Opposite page*
The best of friends – Tommy Smith and his beloved Jay Trump

and when he cocked his ears and pushed and shoved at your pockets, he could, in the words of Brian Delaney, who later became his lad, 'charm the heart out of you!'

Slow, patient work in the schooling ring had brought results and Jay Trump began to look like a real racehorse. The fat became muscle; the well-proportioned workmanlike look, characterised by his deep girth and great sweep of shoulders, slowly became apparent, and Jay Trump would do anything his rider asked him. I decided that Tommy and Jay Trump would make their English debut at Sandown in the Autumn Trial over 3 miles on 21 October. There were just two opponents, the favourite, Comforting Wave and a relatively unknown horse, Can Go. Tommy travelled in the horse box with Jay Trump and I reminded him, 'Jay Trump isn't fit yet, this is just a school, give him a good trip and a pleasant experience.'

I told Tommy to stay on the inside and try to keep a horse alongside. I felt he'd jump quicker that way over unfamiliar fences. I didn't want him to be alone, I wanted him in touch going up the rise, for Tommy to kick on there; if he was on his own at the last, he'd be inclined to steady himself and lose precious ground. Tommy did it splendidly, hugging the rail all the way round and winning by five lengths—my first success as a trainer, Tommy had won on his first ride in England, and Jay Trump was qualified for Aintree.

It was uncanny the way Tommy had carried out my instructions. It was almost as if I had ridden the race myself and it was an experience that was going to be repeated at Aintree.

The days and weeks raced past with Tommy's dedication and obsession quite unreal. I wanted Jay Trump and Tommy to have more racing experience of English courses and, a month after Sandown, they went to Windsor and won the Brocas Chase; then they were beaten by ten lengths by the brilliant Frenchman's Cove in a two-horse race for the King George VI at Kempton Park on Boxing Day.

Days of fog and snow and freezing weather left Tommy restless and bored during January but I blew my top when he calmly announced that he had made reservations to go skiing at St Moritz. 'Over my dead body,' I told him. 'I'm not going to sit by while you break a leg skiing.' He got the message and so for the next few weeks while Jay Trump was let down, Tommy and Frances made several trips to London to the theatre, or Tommy just rested at home, reading. In truth, I doubt whether he could ever really get the Grand National out of his mind. If ever my wife and I went to dinner with him in the evening, the talk quickly turned to Aintree and Nationals past. In February, the work began in earnest . . .

Tommy and Jay Trump went to Newbury and won the Harwell Amateur Riders Handicap over 3 miles on 19 February before finishing fifth in the Royal Porcelain Handicap at Worcester on 17 March, just ten days before the National, when the horse was possibly a shade off colour.

It wasn't just the defeat which worried me. One by one, my horses had gone down with the cough and I moved Jay Trump into total isolation in Dyer's Yard across from Kapal Cottage; I did not go near the horse after the Worcester race in case I carried the germ on my clothes. Tommy hardly left Jay Trump's side, only handing over to a security guard at seven o'clock each night. He disinfected everything in sight; Jay Trump's temperature was taken several times a day; his quarters swabbed with disinfectant; when the blacksmith came to shoe him, he was asked to walk in a box filled with antiseptic powder and dip his hands and tools in strong disinfectant.

Tommy alone cared for his horse until the day of the race, mucking out, dressing, feeding, exercising him. Jay Trump missed the bustle of Uplands but Tommy teased him, talked with him and simply played with him to keep him occupied. All this had a marked physical effect on Tommy; he lost weight, couldn't sleep and his sinuses flared up, and the bookmakers who, in February, had made Jay Trump 12–1 favourite for the National, pushed his price out to 25–1. The pressure was intense.

Tommy had made sure he was as fit as could be: he did not drink and smoked very little and his normal weight of 10st 5 lbs was well within the 11st 5 lbs Jay Trump had been set to carry at Aintree. Still Tommy kept to a careful diet, eating almost as many carrots as Jay Trump, and he was a common sight pedalling along on his bike, doing almost twenty miles a day.

Bryan Marshall and I tutored him on the use of the whip though, to be fair, Jay Trump did not need the whip. Tommy was one-handed and we got him carrying his whip while cycling, moving it from hand to hand and hitting the bike as he rode imaginary finishes. Night after night, he sat on a straight-backed chair transferring his whip back and forth as he sent the chair galloping across the floor. And we coached him how to ride a finish. Keith Piggott had films of five years of Grand Nationals. I studied them with Tommy over and over again, backwards and forwards in slow motion; I pointed out the position I had been in during each phase of the race and told him why. I told him over and over again that there was always room for horses on the inside; that was the way I wanted him to go at Aintree. Not only is it the shortest distance but you generally avoided being brought down. I'd had fourteen rides in the National and won it twice. I did my best to pass on what I had learned, not that I could have had a better pupil. Tommy ate, slept and drank the National, and by now I was well and truly caught up in his enthusiasm.

Fred Winter greets
Jay Trump after the
triumph in the 1965
Grand National

Fred Winter greets Jay Trump after the triumph in the 1965 Grand National

Then came National Week itself and Tommy's first look at the greatest steeplechase course in the world. I could sense surprise in his eyes; it *was* bigger and tougher than even he had imagined. Five times he walked the course. I felt Jay Trump's ace was his jumping, only doubting whether he would be fast enough for the race. I told Tommy, 'Ride the race the way Jay Trump wants it to be ridden, not the way everybody else is riding; go at a pace and take up a position most advantageous to him. Don't go too fast too soon, stay out of danger—and stay on the inside.'

The Canal Turn, I decided, would be the most crucial fence of all; it was made for Jay Trump and Tommy could utilise his natural inclination to jump left. 'Take him out towards the centre,' I told him, 'and let him jump across at an angle. So long as you don't get any interference, you'll save valuable ground and when you're over The Canal second time around, it's time to think about making the best of your way home.'

Someone had asked Tommy the day before the race how he felt. 'Horrified, just horrified!' He went off to the cinema that afternoon to see a war film starring Frank Sinatra. It's title: *None But The Brave*. The atmosphere all around him was tense and strained; the horse's owner Mrs Stephenson had come over from Ohio and Tommy's mother, Margot, had come from Warrenton, Virginia. Tommy and Frances escaped the attention of the Press and the late-night revellers by booking themselves into a small hotel where he hoped to get some sleep before the Great Day.

Tommy rode Jay Trump onto the course for a little trot at eight o'clock on the Saturday morning. When he pulled up after a brief canter from The Chair to the water jump, the horse wasn't blowing enough to put out the match to my cigarette. Our luck had held; Jay Trump wasn't coughing, his temperature was normal, the course, saturated earlier in the week by rain and snow, was drying up and the going would be to Jay Trump's liking. There was nothing more to do but wait, that long agonising wait I had known so well in my own riding days. Now Tommy Smith, who almost seemed a part of me, was about to make the journey I knew so well.

But was he really up to the demands of The Greatest Steeplechase in the World after just five rides in England? There is nothing like the National and with forty-six opponents and four and a half miles to travel I would have been happy for him and Jay Trump just to survive. Survival alone was not on Tommy Smith's agenda; he was going out there to win and nothing else.

The race itself was remarkable—I could hardly believe my eyes. Tommy and Jay Trump, jumping as magnificently as I hoped they would, were at the exact place I wanted them at every crucial point of the race. Tommy took his time and dropped Jay Trump out in the early stages and then picked up his ground exactly as I wanted him to. He was riding a copybook race.

With three fences to go, they began a long drawn-out tussle with Pat McCarron and Freddie, the 7–2 favourite. Neither rider, neither horse yielded an inch, giving the crowd as fine a spectacle as any National had ever produced. They raced within a length of each other, well clear of the only other twelve horses still standing as they came back on to the racecourse for the last time.

Jay Trump put in a magnificent jump at the final fence to land slightly in front and Tommy drove him more than a length clear. However, Freddie,

who was conceding us 5 lbs, was almost at Jay Trump's side by the elbow and for a moment I feared that all Tommy's hopes were to be shattered on that run-in of so many broken dreams. For the one and only time, Tommy almost panicked, picking up his stick. He gave Jay Trump one crack and was about to deliver a second when halfway through the stroke, as if by telepathy, reading my own mind, he put it down and Jay Trump ran on to win by three-quarters of a length to ensure Tommy Smith a well-earned place in history—the first American to ride the winner of the Grand National. And victory for me with my first runner in the race. My overwhelming memory, though, is the uncanny way Tommy rode the race; it was a virtual replica of my successful ride on Kilmore in 1962. A dream race if ever I saw one.

*Opposite page*
Jay Trump, the horse who made it all come true for Tommy Smith, is the toast of Uplands, Lambourn, after Aintree

# General Index

Page numbers in *italic* refer to illustrations

Allen, Myrtle, 103
Allen, Yas, 103–4
Aly Khan, Prince, 122
Ancil, Derek, 37, 138
**Ascot Gold Cup (1963)**, 110–15
**Ascot Gold Cup (1980)**, 27–32
Assheton-Smith, Sir Charles, 121
Astor, Lord, 20
**Ayr Gold Cup (1973)**, 144–7

Balding, Emma, 13, 16
**Balding, Ian**, 10–19: *18*
Balding, Toby, 12
Barron, Tommy, 68–9
Barry, Ron, 73
Bartholomew, Mick, 103
Baxter, Geoff, 25
Beasley, Bobby, 37, 137–8: *139*
Beatty, Peter, 150
**Beech Open Novices' Chase (1979)**, 61–7
Belper, Lord, 130, 133
Biddle, Mrs, 155
Biddlecombe, Terry, 140–2
Blackstead, Mr, 134
Boult, Rodney, 52: *51*
Boussaffa, Amar, 92
Boyd-Rochfort, Sir Cecil, 32
Bradley, Rodney, 52
Brain, Geoffrey, 63
Breasley, Scobie, 128, 130
Brittain, Clive, 165
Brooke, Geoffrey, 155
Brookshaw, Tim, 137
Brown, Alan, 42, 161
Brown, Jock, 146, 148
Bruce, Hervey, 33–4
Brudenell-Bruce, Dana, 58–9
**Budgett, Arthur**, 20–6: *21*

Budgett, Bay, 26
Budgett, Christopher, 26
Bullock, Johnny, 118
Burch, Preston, 11
Burke, John, 143: *142*
Burkhart, John, 110
Butters, Frank, 152
Byrne, Paddy, 123
Byrne, Willie, 123

Candy, Mr & Mrs Derrick, 162
Carberry, Tommy, 105–6
Carmody, Tommy, 39–43
Carson, Willie, 163
Carter, Tommy, 14
Cauthen, Steve, 97, 99–102: *101*
Carver, Leonard, 134–7
Carver, Mrs, 135–7
**Cecil, Henry**, 27–32, 165: *28*
**Cesarewitch (1966)**, 128–33
Chalmers, Snowy, 104
Chambers, Tony, 140
Champion, Bob, 68, 71, 75, 77–9: *70, 80*
**Cheltenham Gold Cup (1979)**, 55–60
**Cheltenham Gold Cup (1982)**, 38–47
Clayton, Jack, 152
Clifford-Turner, Raymond, 144–7
Cockburn, Bay, 105–7
Connolly, Michael, 92
Cook, Paul, 145
Cooper, Graham, 63, 67
Costello, Paddy, 172
Coulthwaite, Tom, 135
Court, Monty, 78
**Crump, Neville**, 33–7: *35*

d'Alassio, Carlo, 27
Datessen, Christian, 92

Dawbin, Jack, 104
de Chambure, Comte Roland, 91
de Rothschild, Baron Guy, 20
Deacon, Harry, 20
Delahooke, James, 83
Delaney, Brian, 180
**Derby (1973)**, 20–6
**Derby (1975)**, 162–9
Derby, Lord, 167
Devonshire, Duchess of, 122
Dick, Dave, 135–7: *136*
**Dickinson, Michael**, 38–47: *47*
Dickinson, Monica, 38, 47
Dickinson, Tony, 38, 47
Doleuze, Georges, 93
Dorsett, Ken, 62, 67
Dowdeswell, Tom, 23
Doyle, Jack, 124, 127
Doyle, Paul, 38
Dreaper, Jim, 105
**Dunlop, John**, 48–54: *51*
Durr, Frankie, 22–3, 145

Eagles, Brian, 82
Earnshaw, Robert, 39, 43–6: *47*
**Easterby, Peter**, 47, 55–60: *59*
Eddery, Pat, 25, 163, 166–9: *168*
Edwards, Josephine, 83
Eldin, Eric, 130
Elizabeth, H.M. Queen, 83, 90, 136, 167–8
Elizabeth the Queen Mother, H.M. Queen, 69, 123, 135–7, 161: *47, 160*
Embiricos, Nick, 69, 71–5, 77–8, 81
Embiricos, Valda, 70–3, 75, 78, 81

Fairbairn, George, 142
Feather, Christine, 39–42
Fenwick, Bobby, 177
Ferris, Ann, 106, 108–9:
    107, 108
Firestone, Bertram, 170,
    172
Flippance, Fred, 145
Forster, Tim, 61–7, 103:
    62
Foster, George, 43, 45
Francis, Dick, 136
Francome, John, 44–5,
    143, 161: 65
Frank, Charles, 165
Freeguard, Steve, 82
Freeman, Keith, 162–3

Gaslee, Nick, 162, 167
Gifford, Althea, 68, 73, 75,
    78–80
Gifford, Josh, 68–81, 82:
    70, 76, 80
Gifford, Nicholas, 79
Gould, Malcolm, 52
Grand National (1948),
    33–6
Grand National (1956),
    134–7
Grand National (1961),
    134, 137–8
Grand National (1964),
    116–32
Grand National (1965),
    176–85
Grand National (1970),
    134, 140–2
Grand National (1976),
    134, 142–3
Grand National (1981),
    68–81
Griffin, Bob, 125
Griffin, Joe, 118–19,
    121–2
Guy, Derek, 25

Halifax, Lady Ruth, 50–3
Halifax, (late) Lord, 48,
    50–3
Hallum, John, 11–12,
    15–16
Harwood, Guy, 50, 77,
    82–90: 84

Hastings-Bass, William, 16
Head, Alec, 18, 92–4
Head, Criquette, 91–6: 94,
    95
Head, Freddie, 91–6: 94
Head, Ghislaine, 91–2, 96
Henderson, Nicky, 79
Herbert, Ivor, 137
Hern, Dick, 13, 81, 84, 128
Hide, Edward, 25: 24
Hills, Barry, 97–102: 98
Hills, Penny, 102
Hindley, Jeremy, 144
Hobbs, Bruce, 49
Hogan, Pat, 97
Holleran, Michael, 172
Holliday, Lionel, 20
Hughes, Dessie, 106, 123,
    125, 127: 126
Humphreys, John, 62
Hutchinson, Ron, 49–50
Hyde, Tim, 116

Irwin, Lady (present Lady
    Halifax), 52
Irwin, Lord (present Lord
    Halifax), 48, 52–3
Irish Derby (1978), 48–54
Irish Sweeps Handicap
    Hurdle (1979), 103–9

Jarvis, Jack, 104
Jennings, Bill, 16
Joel, Stanhope, 56, 58
Johnson, Charlie, 169
Johnson, Ernie, 25, 99, 146
Johnson Houghton, Helen,
    163

Kelleway, Paul, 130
Keogh, Joan, 108
Keogh, Moya, 116, 118
Keogh, Raymond, 103–9
Kirby, Tony, 25

Laing, Ray, 169
Lamb, Ridley, 37
Lane, Harry, 37
Lawson, Geoff, 82, 87
Lewis, Geoff, 13–15,
    18–19, 113, 115: 17
Lindley, Jimmy, 152–3,
    155
Loughbridge, Sam, 156–7,
    159–60

Magnier, John, 99
Maguire, Jack, 157
Marshall, Bryan, 119–20,
    181: 121
Maughan, Peter, 25
Maxwell, Bob, 23
Maxwell, Diana, 23
Maxwell, Wynnie, 23
McCalmont, Victor, 52
McCarron, Pat, 183
McCormack, Matt, 169
McGowan, Anne Marie,
    124
McGowan, Joe, 124
Mellon, Paul, 11–12, 14,
    16, 19, 56
Mellor, Stan, 37, 137
Mercer, Joe, 28, 30, 150,
    166: 31
Mercer, Syd, 134
Messer, Fred, 130
Mewies, Jack, 39
Mills, Phyllis, 176
Minton, David, 149
Molony, Tim, 135
Moore, Arthur, 103–9:
    108
Moore, Dan, 103–4, 109,
    176
Moore, Joan, 103, 109
Moore, Mary, 103, 107,
    109
Morby, Frank, 166
Morrissey, Paddy, 127
Muinos, Andry, 82–3
Muinos, Max, 82: 88
Muldoon, John, 172
Mulhern, John, 127
Murless, Sir Noel, 110–15:
    111

Niarchos, Stavros, 128, 130
Nicholson, David, 79, 157
Nickalls, Tom, 111
Norfolk, Lavinia Duchess
    of, 50, 52, 152

Oaks (1981), 170–5
O'Brien, Phonsie, 118–20:
    119
O'Brien, Vincent, 85,
    98–9, 116–22: 117
O'Donoghue, Jack, 118

Oliver, Rowley, 134
**O'Toole, Mick**, 106, 123–7, 157: *124*
O'Neill, Jonjo, 57–8: *59*
Outon, Snowy, 102
Oxley, John, 50

Palmer, Bill, 12, 15
Peacock, Matt, 33
Pelham, Henry, 79
Perkins, Reginald, 95
Permin, Jorgen, 91
Perrett, Mark, 87
Pfaff, Arthur, 91
Piggott, Keith, 25, 181
Piggott, Lester, 19, 25, 29–30, 113–15, 146, 172, 175: *112, 114, 173, 174*
Pitt, Arthur, 143
Pope, Michael, 151
Porchester, Lord, 90
Powell, Brian, 38, 45
Pratt, Bill, 55
Pratt, Lord Michael, 63, 67
Prendergast, Paddy, 152
**Price, Ryan**, 99, 104, 128–33: *129, 132*
Pritchard-Gordon, Gavin, 149
**Prix de l'Arc de Triomphe (1971)**, 14–19
**Prix de l'Arc de Triomphe (1979)**, 91–6
Proctor, John, 34–5

Raymond, 'Teasy Weasy', 142–3
Redmond, Tony, 124
Reilly, Tom, 16
Rennison, Graham, 46
Richards, Sir Gordon, 128
Rickaby, Bill, 111
**Rimell, Fred**, 105, 134–43: *142*
Rimell, Mercy, 134, 137–8
Robinson, Nicholas, 97
Roger-Smith, Mr, 68–9, 81
Rohan, Pat, 144
Rooney, Willie, 106
Rosebery, Lord, 116
Rowe, Richard, 73
Ryan, Matty, 109

Sassoon, Lady, 113
Sassoon, Sir Victor, 110, 113
Saunders, Dick, 67
Scarf, Robert, 172
Scott, Gerry, 37
Scudamore, Michael, 37
Sefton, Lord, 113
Sensenich, Jay, 177
Shead, Tony, 97, 99
Sheriffe, Monica, 151–2
Shiltston, Stuart, 157
Shoemaker, Bill, 102
Slack, George, 121
Sleator, Paddy, 125
Smith, Bill, 157, 159–61
Smith, Crompton, 179
Smith, Doug, 113, 128, 131–3, 144: *129*
Smith, Eph, 128
Smith, Frances, 176–7, 179–80, 183
Smith, Kitty, 179
Smith, Swank, 33
**Smith, Tommy**, 176–85: *178, 184*
Smith, Worcester, 179
Smyly, David, 61–3
Smyly, Mark, 167
Smyly, Patricia, 63–4, 67
Stack, Tommy, 42
Starkey, Greville, 50, 53–4, 82, 85–6, 89–90: *88*
Stephenson, Mary, 177, 183
Stephenson, Willie, 135
Stirk, Anthony, 45
Stoute, Pat, 114–15, 149
**Stoute, Michael**, 144–7: *148*
Sturman, Ted, 104
**Sun Alliance Novices' Hurdle (1975)**, 123–7
Swinburn, Wally (Snr), 171–2, 175

Taaffe, Pat, 140–1: *141*
Tate, Thomas, 39
Taylor, Brian, 166
Thompson, Arthur, 34, 36–7: *36*
Thomson Jones, Harry, 144–5

Thorne, John, 80
Thorner, Graham, 57, 64: *65*
Toppin, James, 116
Towers-Clark, Peter, 20
Townsend, Tom, 82
Treacy, Sean, 106
**Tree, Jeremy**, 150–5: *153*
Tuchy, Christie, 120
**Two Thousand Guineas (1963)**, 150–5
**Two Thousand Guineas (1979)**, 97–102
**Two Thousand Guineas (1981)**, 82–90

van Cutsem, Mimi, 176
Vaughan, Jeremy, 137–8
Vittadini, Dr Carlo, 162–3, 165–6, 168: *168*

Walwyn, Cath, 160
**Walwyn, Fulke**, 156–61: *160*
**Walwyn, Peter**, 28, 49, 162–9: *164*
Walwyn, Virginia, 162, 166
Ward, Liam, 155
Warden, Dick, 150
Warner, Ron, 82
Wates, Andrew, 103
Watkinson, Ian, 40
Weedy, Mick, 16
Welbourne, Alan, 29
**Weld, Dermot**, 97, 170–5: *171*
Wertheimer, Jacques, 95
Whelan, Bill, 151–2
Whelan, Dermot 'Boggy', 166, 175
Whelehan, Mick, 157
**Whitbread Gold Cup (1981)**, 156–61
Whitney, Jock, 153
Whyte, Kevin, 39, 45
Williams, Gary, 46
Wilson, E.P., 121
Wilson, Jock, 130
Wilson, Julian, 23, 26
**Winter, Fred**, 176–85: *182*
Wright, Percy, 23

Yule, Gladys, 151

Zilber, Maurice, 91

# INDEX OF HORSES

Abbeydale, 99
Alberoni, 120: *121*
Alcoa, 128
**Aldaniti**, 68–81, 123: *70, 76, 80*
Aldie, 15–16
All Found, 130–1
Allez France, 92
Alphadamus, 146
**Alverton**, 40, 55–60, 72, 78, 156: *57, 59*
Alvertona, 55
Alycidon, 110, 113
Americos, 98–9
Anaglogs Daughter, 42, 157
Anglo, 179
Anifa, 32
Anna's Prince, 59
Anne's Pretender, 167
Antique, 104
Antler, 28
Archive, 38
Arctic Air, 124–5
Arctique Royal, 172
Ardar, 84
Ardfield, 104
Ardross, 30
Argument, 96
Arkle, 38
Assad, 140
Aureole, 38
Avon's Pride, 128
Ayala, 142
Azuline, 170

Bachelor's Hall, 71
Badanloch, 37
Badsworth, Boy, 43
Bahram, 152
Ballymoss, 144
Balto, 114
Bay Lancer, 128
Be Trump, 177
Bel Bolide, 90
Ben Nevis, 67
Betton Grose, 160
Bidar, 134
Big Pal, 84
Bilbo Baggins, 124

Blakeney, 20, 22, 25, 162
Blessed Again, 144
**Blue Cashmere**, 144–7: *147, 148*
Blue Peter, 20, 116
**Blue Wind**, 170–5: *173, 174*
Bobjob, 160
Bois Roussel, 150
Bolak, 49
Bold Raider, 84
Bolide, 98
Bolkonski, 99, 165
Border Incident, 41–2
Borealis, 151
Borobella, 150–1
Bregawn, 38, 45–6: *44*
Brigadier Gerard, 13
Bright Beam, 14–15
Bright Finish, 150
Bright Highway, 104
Broomfield, 118
Brother Will, 43
Brown Lad, 58
Bruni, 166
Buckskin, 28–9

Cairn Rouge, 84
Campton, 84
Can Go, 180
Caro, 14
Cat O'Mountaine, 97
Cavo Doro, 25
C.E.D., 131–2
Chamos, 56
Chanteur, 151
Chinrullah, 42, 106, 109
Chorus Beauty, 20
Church Parade, 83–4
Churchtown, 120
Citissima, 172
Clear Verdict, 84
Comforting Wave, 180
Condessa, 175
Constans, 150
Copper Kiln, 106
Corby, 164, 166
Cottage, 33
Court Martial, 150, 170
Covertcoat, 121

Cracaval, 102
Crepello, 110–11, 113
Crepuscule, 110
Crocket, 155
Croghan Hill, 170
Croque Monsieur, 30
Cunard, 49

David Jack, 124
**Davy Lad**, 69, 123–7: *126*
Deep Gale, 109
Derek H, 68
Derrinstown, 118
Detroit, 96
Devon Loch, 135–6
**Diamond Edge**, 42, 57, 156–61: *158*
Dickens Hill, 99, 127
Double Bore, 150–1
Double Jump, 150
Dozo, 140
Dramatist, 124
Dual, 92
Dunette, 92–3
D'Urberville, 150

Early Mist, 116, 119–20
Ela-Mana-Mou, 82–3, 95–6
Electrify, 103
Elizabeth Wales, 145
Ellangowan, 116
English Summer, 134
**E.S.B.**, 122, 134–7, 138: *136*
Exclusive Native, 96
Exdirectory, 53–4: *53*
Express Mail, 69, 123
Eyecatcher, 143

Fabulous Dancer, 95
Fair Selina, 144
Fancy Free, 20
Father Delaney, 161: *158*
Fighting Fit, 72
Fireside Chat, 12
First of the Dandies, 34
Flocon, 151
**Forbidden Fruit**, 61–7: *65, 66*

Fort Devon, 71
Francesco, 29
Freddie, 183, 185
Freebooter, 37
Freefoot, 25
French Excuse, 141
Frenchman's Cove, 180
Fresh Winds, 138

Gaffer, 58
Gaul, 113, 115
Gay Heather, 118
Gay Mecene, 95
**Gay Trip**, 134, 137,
    140–2: *141*
Gayshuka, 170
Gazpacho, 152
Gentle Moya, 136
Golden Miller, 138
Good Days, 116
Grand Mieuxce, 110
Great Nephew, 163
Green Dancer, 164, 167
Green God, 12
Grittar, 67
**Grundy**, 13, 162–9: *167,
    168*

Happy Home, 34
Hardiemma, 48
Hartstown, 124
Hatton's Grace, 116
Hawaiian Sound, 50, 53
Henbit, 84
Hethersett, 20
Highway Patt, 156
Home Guard, 146
Honey Parrot, 163
Honeylight, 110
Honour Bound, 156
Hornbeam, 20
Hugh Lupus, 110
Hula Dancer, 155

Ile de Bourbon, 50
Imposant, 138
Inkerman, 53
Inventory, 127
Ionian, 155: *154*
**Irian**, 103–9: *107, 108*
Irish Lizard, 135

Jack of Trumps, 41, 124

Jan Ekels, 82
Jan Stewer, 63
Jay Trump, 176–85: *178,
    182, 184*
Jerry M, 121
Jimuru, 138
John Cherry, 150
Jonjo, 138
Juliette Marny, 150
Julio Mariner, 28

Kalaglow, 85
Kashmir II, 144–5
Kassak, 98
Kelso Chant, 39
Kilijaro, 97
Kilkilwell, 75
Kilmore, 74, 138, 185
Kind of Hush, 86
Known Fact, 150
Kris, 30, 160–2
Ksar, 22, 25

Labienus, 49
Lake City, 99
Lanecourt, 175
Larbawn, 161
Le Daim, 34
Le Marmot, 91
**Le Moss**, 27–32: *30, 31*
Leap Lively, 175
Legal Joy, 37, 116, 119
Legal Switch, 103
L'Escargot, 103, 140
Levmoss, 27
Life Sentence, 150–1
Light Cavalry, 30
Linden Tree, 13, 162
Little Owl, 43, 45, 58, 77
Lord Gayle, 170
Lord George, 104–5
Love Apple, 62
Lovely Cottage, 33
Lucius, 58
Lyphard, 92

Mabel, 162
Madam Gay, 175: *173*
Major Thompson, 58–9
Man of Harlech, 50, 52
Mark Anthony, 165–6
Master Monday, 109
Master Smudge, 41

Master Willie, 84
Mattaboy, 90
Mayday Melody, 146
Merryman II, 37, 138
Michael Andrew, 82
Midnight Marauder, 150
Midsummer Night II, 56
Milan Mill, 11
Miletus, 153
**Mill Reef**, 10–19, 48, 162:
    *10, 17, 18*
Mintmaster, 131
Miss Dawn, 131–2
Miss Hunter, 140–1
Miss McTaffy, 163
Misti IV, 114
Mon Fils, 25
Monksfield, 58
Monsanto, 166
Monterrico, 114
Morris Dancer, 15
**Morston**, 20–6: *21, 24*
Mr Know All, 125
My Flame, 137
My Swallow, 12–13

Nadjar, 84
Nearco, 103, 128
Never Bend, 11
Nickel Coin, 116, 118
**Nicolaus Silver**, 37, 134,
    137–8: *139*
Night Nurse, 40–3, 45,
    58–9, 159
Nijinsky, 13, 15
No Alimony, 163–4, 166
No Argument, 61–2
No Justice, 140
Nonoalca, 92–3
North Stoke, 49–50
Northern Dancer, 92

O'Malley Point, 138
**Only For Life**, 150–5: *154*
Ottery News, 161
Overplay, 170

Pampered King, 58
Pandolfi, 56
Parbleu, 149
Parkhill, 124
Party Choice, 130
Persian Gulf, 128

Persian Lancer, 128–33: 129, 132
Persian Road, 150
Pistol Packer, 18
Pitasia, 92, 95
Polygamy, 167
Portway Nick, 41
Prime Boy, 151
Princequillo, 11
Producer, 93
Projector, 22–3, 25
Prominent King, 58
Promptitude, 134
Purdo, 40

Quantico, 11
Quare Times, 116
Quentin, 151
Quiet Fling, 150

Rag Trade, 134, 142–3: 142
Ragusa, 20, 97
Rambling Artist, 58
Rankin, 84, 87
Rathgorman, 43, 46
R. B. Chesne, 102
Recitation, 82, 85, 87, 89
Red Ray, 11
Red Reef, 12
Red Regent, 166–7
Red Rum, 143
Romaunt, 125
Roquefort, 121
Ros Rock, 152–3
Royal Charley, 75
Royal Judgement, 73
Royal Mail, 58, 72, 79
Royal Mannacle, 99
Royal Tan, 116–22, 136: 117, 119, 121
Russian Hero, 118

Sallust, 97
Salpinx, 92, 95
Sandy Creek, 99
Scintillate, 94, 150
Scottish Flight II, 138
Sea Bird, 13

Sea Pigeon, 55, 58
Sealy, 93
Sexton Blake, 49
Shannon Lass, 36
Sharpo, 150
Sheila, 33
Sheila's Cottage, 33–7: 35, 36
Shergar, 13, 144, 146, 175
Shirley Heights, 48–54: 51, 53
Shoemaker, 162
Shuilaris, 105
Silver Buck, 38–47, 75: 44
Silver Cloud, 38
Silver Fame, 34
Sir Gaylord, 170
Sir Montagu, 56
Six of Diamonds, 156
Spartan Missile, 80
Spree, 150, 152–3, 155
Square Deal, 130
Steel Heart, 163
Sticky Case, 170
Stonepark, 78
Storm Bird, 85
Straight Row, 57, 105–6, 109
Summer Knave, 145
Sundew, 135
Sunset Cristo, 42, 45–6
Sunyboy, 69, 123, 127
Sweet Joe, 56
Sweet September, 41
Swing Easy, 150

Taher, 90
Taine, 114–15
Tall Noble, 125
Tap On Wood, 97–102: 100, 101
Taros, 168
Tartan, 116
Teal, 37, 116, 119
Ten Dollars More, 67
The Otter, 140
Three Roses, 92
Three Troikas, 91–6: 93, 94, 95

Tiber, 150
Tied Cottage, 41–2, 46, 58, 75, 125, 127, 156: 57
Tinella, 55
Titus Oates, 140
To-Agori-Mou, 82–90: 87, 88
Tonga Prince, 177
Totowah, 29
Traquair, 50
Tree Tangle, 71
Tristram Shandy, 105
Troy, 13, 91, 127
Tubalcain, 131
Tudor Line, 120–1
Tudor Music, 83
Twilight Alley, 110–15: 112, 114
Twinburn, 109: 107
Two of Diamonds, 102

Utrillo, 128

Villay, 140
Vincent, 30
Voluptuary, 121
Vulgan, 140
Vulture, 141

Waterway, 92
Wayward Lad, 44
Well To Do, 67, 142
Whitstead, 50
Willie Wumpkins, 58
Windmill Girl, 20, 26
Within The Law, 58
Word From Lundy, 163
Workman, 33
Wyndburgh, 138

Yellow Dean, 106
Young Generation, 82–3, 101: 100

Zahia, 34
Zhetaire, 92
Zongalero, 79